OCEAN WARRIORS

The Thrilling Story of the 2001/2002 Volvo Ocean Race Round the World

ROB MUNDLE

HarperSports

An imprint of HarperCollins*Publishers*

Harper*Sports*
An imprint of HarperCollins*Publishers*

First published in Australia in 2002
by HarperCollins*Publishers* Pty Limited
ABN 36 009 913 517
A member of the HarperCollins*Publishers* (Australia) Pty Limited Group
www.harpercollins.com.au

Copyright © Rob Mundle 2002

The right of Rob Mundle to be identified as the moral rights author of this work
has been asserted by him in accordance with the *Copyright Amendment
(Moral Rights) Act 2000* (Cth).

HarperCollins*Publishers*
25 Ryde Road, Pymble, Sydney NSW 2073, Australia
31 View Road, Glenfield, Auckland 10, New Zealand
77–85 Fulham Palace Road, London W6 8JB, United Kingdom
Hazelton Lanes, 55 Avenue Road, Suite 2900, Toronto, Ontario, M5R 3L2
and 1995 Markham Road, Scarborough, Ontario, M1B 5M8, Canada
10 East 53rd Street, New York NY 10022, USA

National Library of Australia Cataloguing-in-publication data:

Mundle, Rob.
Ocean warriors: the thrilling story of the 2001/2002 Volvo
Ocean Race round the world.
ISBN 0 7322 7238 6.
1. Volvo Ocean Race. 2. Yachting. I. Title.
797.1246

Front cover image by Richard Langdon/Ocean Images
Back cover images all by Rick Tomlinson, except for top left by Daniel Forster, *illbruck*
and author picture by Richard Langdon/Ocean Images
Map, cutaway drawing and statistics courtesy of Volvo Ocean Race
Cover and internal design by Louise McGeachie, HarperCollins Design Studio
Printed and bound in Australia by Griffin Press on 79gsm Bulky Paperback White

5 4 3 2 1   02 03 04 05

ROB MUNDLE is the author of the highly acclaimed international bestseller *Fatal Storm*, the story of the tragic 1998 Sydney to Hobart yacht race.

Born in Sydney, Australia, he started his career in the local office of the blossoming national daily newspaper *The Australian*, as its first cadet journalist. After training as a general reporter he combined his career with his favourite sport, becoming a specialist sailing reporter. He is recognised in Australia, and internationally, as a leading media authority on sailing.

He has won local, state and Australian championships and contested many major international offshore events.

Beyond the field of journalism he was responsible for the introduction and highly successful marketing and promotion of the Laser and J/24 classes in Australia.

In the 1980s he established a career in television as a reporter, commentator and, at one stage, a primetime news weatherman. He has reported on six America's Cup matches (including the live international coverage of Australia's historic win in 1983), four Olympics and numerous other major races, including the annual Sydney to Hobart classic.

In 1993 his media and event management company, Rob Mundle Promotions, was contracted by the five-star Hayman Island Resort to organise events. Hayman Island Yacht Club was formed on behalf of the resort and in 1995 staged the inaugural Hayman Island Big Boat Series. It was acclaimed as one of the best regattas of its type in the world.

For more than a decade he has been actively involved with the Cure Cancer Australia Foundation, contributing to the raising of over $1 million for the foundation.

As well as staging events and handling corporate PR, Rob Mundle writes for magazines around the world. His first book, the biography *Sir James Hardy: An Adventurous Life*, written in 1993, was a bestseller.

This book is dedicated to the world's ocean warriors.

You dare to live our dreams.

Contents

The Route   iix

The Yachts   ix

The *Team News Corp* Crew   x

The Skippers   xii

Acknowledgments   xiii

Introduction   1

Prelude   3

The Launching Pad   10

The Countdown   24

LEG ONE > Southampton to Cape Town   32

LEG TWO > Cape Town to Sydney   64

LEG THREE > Sydney to Hobart to Auckland   94

LEG FOUR > Auckland to Rio de Janeiro   116

LEG FIVE > Rio de Janeiro to Miami   142

LEG SIX > Miami to Baltimore   162

LEG SEVEN > Annapolis to La Rochelle   178

LEG EIGHT > La Rochelle to Gothenburg   192

LEG NINE > Gothenburg to Kiel   206

Epilogue   220

Leaderboard   222

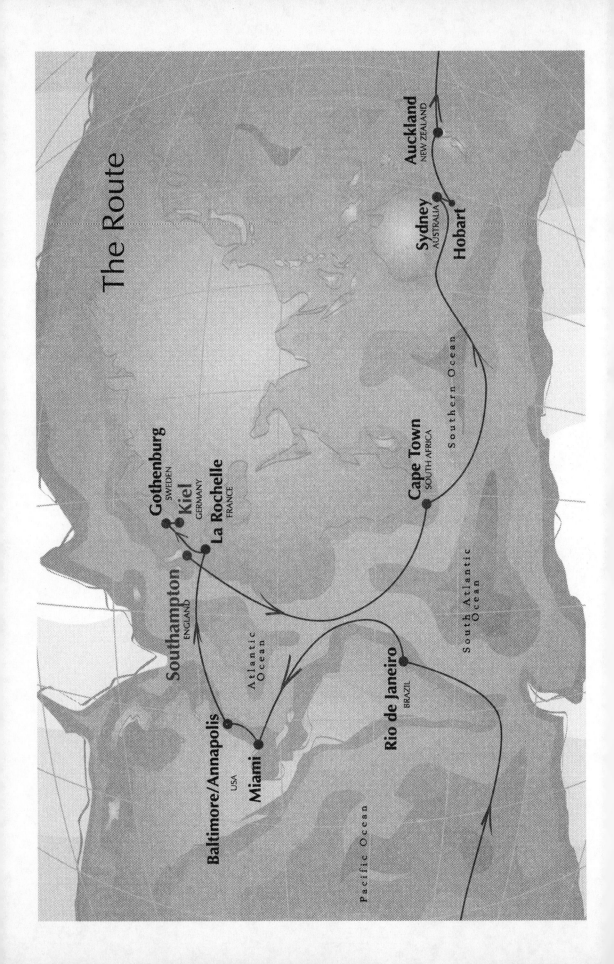

The Route

Gothenburg
SWEDEN
Kiel
GERMANY
La Rochelle
FRANCE
Southampton
ENGLAND

Baltimore/Annapolis
USA
Miami

Atlantic
Ocean

Rio de Janeiro
BRAZIL

Cape Town
SOUTH AFRICA

Southern Ocean

South Atlantic
Ocean

Sydney
AUSTRALIA
Hobart

Auckland
NEW ZEALAND

Pacific Ocean

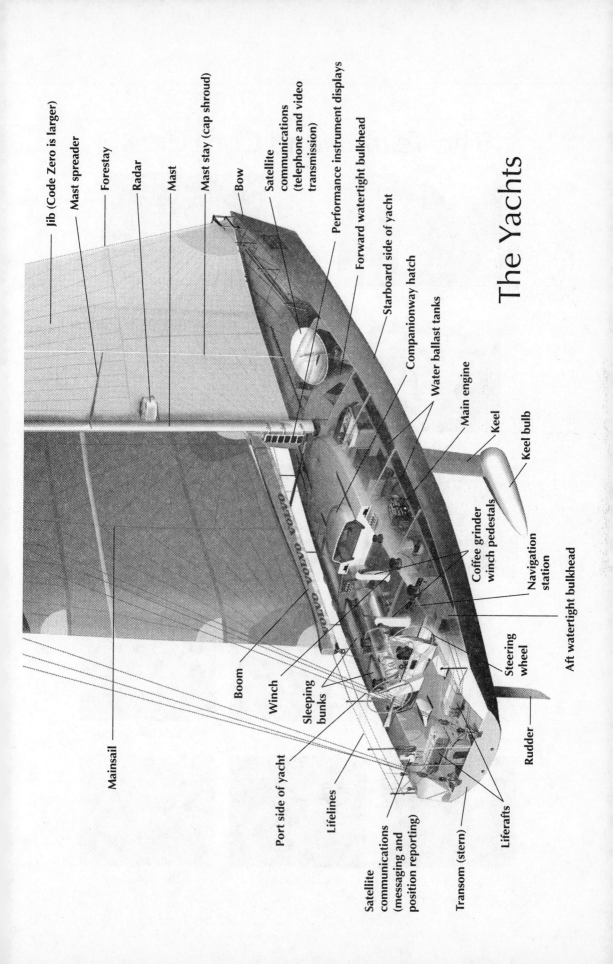

The Yachts

Jib (Code Zero is larger)

Mast spreader

Forestay

Radar

Mast

Mast stay (cap shroud)

Bow

Satellite communications (telephone and video transmission)

Performance instrument displays

Forward watertight bulkhead

Starboard side of yacht

Companionway hatch

Water ballast tanks

Main engine

Keel

Keel bulb

Coffee grinder winch pedestals

Navigation station

Steering wheel

Aft watertight bulkhead

Rudder

Liferafts

Transom (stern)

Satellite communications (messaging and position reporting)

Lifelines

Port side of yacht

Sleeping bunks

Winch

Boom

Mainsail

The *Team News Corp* Crew

Ross Field

Jez Fanstone

Alistair 'Alby' Pratt

Nick White

Craig 'Smiley' Smith

Stuart Childerley

Peter Isler

Campbell Field

Oli Allard

Warwick 'Wazza' Kerr

Jan van der Lee

Richard Langdon

Bart Simpson

Gordon Maguire

Ian 'Barney' Walker

Matt Humphries

Damien 'Shreda' Duke

Justin Slattery

Peter 'Spike' Dorien

Nigel King

Joe Spooner

Jean-Pierre 'J.P.' Macquet

Leah Fanstone

Ashley Abbott

Jeff 'Scotty' Scott

Jon 'Gundy' Gunderson

Steve Cotton

The Skippers

Jez Fanstone *TEAM NEWS CORP*

John Kostecki *ILLBRUCK CHALLENGE*

Gurra Krantz *TEAM SEB*

Lisa McDonald *AMER SPORTS TOO*

Grant Dalton *AMER SPORTS ONE*

Kevin Shoebridge *TEAM TYCO*

Knut Frostad *DJUICE DRAGONS*

Neal McDonald *ASSA ABLOY*

Acknowledgments

There's probably no other sporting contest on the planet that takes so many competitors so often to the brink of life and death situations as the Volvo Ocean Race (VOR). As a consequence the 2001/2002 contest was almost top heavy with incredible stories of great sporting endeavour.

Ocean Warriors was created to present the most powerful cross-section of those stories; and to get them into print could not have been achieved without the support of many people.

Firstly I must recognise the competing sailors whose spirit of adventure and daring deeds laid the foundation for the story. More specifically I must thank the outstanding men and women of *Team News Corp* who adopted me as part of their 'family' for nine months. In embracing the project and allowing me to enter their inner sanctum I was given the rare opportunity to see the inside operations of a VOR campaign. In particular I must thank campaign manager Ross Field, skipper Jez Fanstone, his wife Leah, Ashley Abbott, Jan van der Lee, and syndicate photographer Richard Langdon for their support. Special mention must go to Spencer Moseska, the Los Angeles-based vice-president of News Corp Marketing who, as the company's VOR project coordinator, went to impressive lengths to ensure I had the best possible access to the *News Corp* team and the race.

The VOR Media Centre was always supportive and my specific thanks go to Mark Howell and Lizzie Green for their efforts. Additional photographs from the VOR's official photographer, Rick Tomlinson, also reinforce the story.

My thanks also go to the team at publishers HarperCollins — Alison Urquhart, Jacquie Brown and Louise McGeachie — who kept me pointed in the right direction.

From my own side of the project I must thank Linda Hamilton-Evans for a superb job with the last-minute proofreading. And life would not have gone anywhere near as smoothly if it wasn't for the dedication and efficiency of my assistant, Nicky Ronalds. She made an important contribution to the book and kept the office fully operational while I was chasing yachts across the world.

The navigator sticks his head up and says, 'Iceberg on the bow, one mile.' You are sailing under spinnaker at more than 20 knots, so you only have about three minutes to get the yacht around it. It's snowing and there's only 400 yards of visibility, so we're navigating by radar. I need to know if I should go to the left or to the right to miss it. The navigator comes back up and says, 'It's on the starboard bow,' then disappears. He reappears to say, 'Second iceberg on the port bow, half a mile.'

I'm saying, 'You are kidding me. Is this the same iceberg? Are they joined? Could this be the one iceberg with two peaks? What's the gap between them?' It's then too late to go either side. We've got a 'berg to the left, a 'berg to the right and we're going through the middle.

One of the younger crew turns around and says, 'What if they are connected?'

I look at him and say, 'Then we're going to die.'

GORDON MAGUIRE — WATCH LEADER, *TEAM NEWS CORP*

Introduction

OCEAN WARRIORS. THAT'S WHAT THEY ARE.

Their bravado and ability to push themselves to the limits of endurance are almost beyond comprehension. And it's all in the name of sport. In fact, what they achieve can make other extreme sports look like a romp in a park.

The men and women who compete have an insatiable appetite for tough competition, danger and the challenge of life-threatening experiences. They must cope with everything that heaven and hell can hurl at them. Raw nerve is an essential part of their kit. Yet in the sporting world they are virtual unknowns: ocean yacht racing is not exactly a high-profile spectator sport.

Theirs is a competition in which they must cover more than 32 000 miles in nine months and conquer the world's oceans. The racing is non-stop — 24 hours a day, seven days a week. On rare occasions they have three hours of uninterrupted sleep. To win the battle they must overcome the mind-bending frustration and oppressive heat of tropical calms. They must also master the white-knuckle terror that comes with a snowstorm-driven blast through a minefield of icebergs deep in the Southern Ocean. They face the full spectrum of the ocean's moods, from tabletop-smooth seas to marauding monsters — waves with near-vertical faces the height of a six-storey building. When these break, the avalanche of white water can easily engulf the yacht and its crew.

Surviving the elements is only part of this game; it's also about beating the opposition. When conditions are at their worst, the competitors' skills require them to balance on a razor's edge between maximum speed and self-destruction.

And what awaits them at the end of this supreme test of endurance and yacht-racing skill? Nothing more than a crystal trophy and the knowledge that, if they win, they are the world's best. There's not one penny of prize money.

Are they mad masochists? They don't think so; well, most of them don't. There are some who hit the dock at the end and vow that they will sit under a tree for the rest of their life.

What follows is more than a story about a yacht race. It's about human endeavour, testing the limits of physical and mental endurance, team cohesion, and racing to the max. It's the story of the fortunes of eight of the best ocean racing teams in the world in the Volvo Ocean Race round the world and, in particular, the highs and lows experienced by one of the crews, *Team News Corp*, as they battle to become the world's best ocean warriors.

Prelude

THREE SAILORS LOST their lives when washed overboard in separate incidents in the first of these fully crewed races around the world, staged in 1973/74. Little wonder back then that when it was all over there were suggestions it would be the last such event.

But for those who completed the course the combination of their spirit of adventure and the formula for the competition proved to be a powerful blend: there was sufficient enthusiasm among competitors and would-be participants to go again four years later. And, most importantly, the sponsor liked it.

The initial concept for what would in 2001/2002 become the Volvo Ocean Race came from Colonel Bill Whitbread, of the Whitbread brewing family, and the Royal Naval Sailing Association's Admiral Otto Steiner, literally over a pint of beer. Titled the Whitbread Race, it would be the first time that a fleet of fully crewed racing yachts had faced the perils of the Southern Ocean.

The inaugural race, which started off Portsmouth in England, attracted a wide cross-section of sailors, from near-novices to some of the world's best. And the yachts differed substantially in size (from 32 feet to 80 feet) and design — from cumbersome cruisers to what were then very modern racers. Fourteen of the 17 starters completed the gruelling course. It was noted when the fleet rounded the world's most notorious point of land, South America's Cape Horn, that they had more than doubled the number of pleasure yachts to have completed that passage.

The race has subsequently been staged every four years and evolved from being little more than a cruising competition to a fiercely contested match-up: a 32 000-mile version of the most intense Saturday-afternoon dinghy race on a local waterway. It has attracted some of the world's most famous sailing names — Dennis Conner, the late Sir Peter Blake, Chay Blyth, Paul Cayard and Grant Dalton.

Like any extreme sport, the elements of danger and high drama have contributed greatly to the race's appeal for both competitors and the international audience, which numbers in the millions. Over the years the race's safety record has improved dramatically, but there will always be close calls. Take, for example, what happened to 31-year-old Australian sailor Alby Pratt in 1997. His moment came in the middle of the night when the 64-foot yacht he was aboard was negotiating a course through Bass Strait, the often dangerous stretch of water separating the Australian mainland and the island state of Tasmania. Suddenly, without warning, death was staring him down, winning the tug of war with the yacht that had just ejected him into the turbulent ocean. He felt as though he was trapped in a giant's hand that was dragging him underwater. 'I thought I was gone,' Pratt recalls. 'I was wrapped up completely inside the sail and knew there was no way out.'

The events as they unfolded were terrifying. Pratt had been on stand-by below deck, off watch and napping, but ready to go should he be needed for a sail change. 'There was quite a big sea running,' he says. 'The boat was pounding a lot and there was plenty of green water coming over the foredeck. We were just spearing through the waves. The call came for a change — we needed something smaller. I went up onto the foredeck to help and clipped my safety harness onto a deck fitting. When we got the old sail down we had to carry it to the back of the boat. I unclipped so I could move aft and, just as I did, we nosed through a solid wave that submerged the bow.'

It was like a submarine doing a crash-dive. With tons of water cascading across the deck there was no way Pratt and his crewmates could contain the huge Kevlar sail. It was no contest. The torrent tore it from their grasp and ripped it away.

As the sail went, it washed over Pratt and wrapped around him in the same way a butcher wraps a side of meat. His rapid exit to the ocean was via the leeward side towards the stern, where the stainless-steel safety rail became just a minor obstruction. The combined force of the wave, the sail and its contents, ripped the rail from its mounts like a twig being snapped from a branch. Pratt was over the side and, within seconds, out of sight of his 11 crewmates.

'Luckily, the sail had a sheet [control rope] on it, which was still attached to the boat. When it went tight the shock load effectively unwrapped the sail and I popped out. The next thing I knew, I'd bobbed to the surface and was watching the white stern light of the boat disappearing into the night.'

If the sheet had not remained attached to the boat or had broken, Pratt would almost certainly have been trapped in his Kevlar cocoon and drowned. Wallowing on the surface and still struggling to stay afloat because of the weight of his waterlogged wet-weather gear, Pratt's fingers fumbled for a pocket containing his one hope for salvation: his small but powerful personal strobe light. He found it and with profound relief he pressed the switch and it burst into brightness. In the meantime, the highly experienced crew on the yacht were initiating a rescue procedure they had rehearsed for a moment like this. Within seven minutes they had turned the yacht back, targeted the bright, flashing light they could see each time Pratt crested a wave, sailed to the point, then grabbed their soggy crewmate and dragged him back on deck.

The incident didn't deter Pratt, who completed the race to the finish in England. And he was enlisted as a member of the *News Corp* team for 2001/2002 for his third circumnavigation.

The Volvo Ocean Race crews don't enter the race under the premise that, if trouble strikes, commercial shipping or a nearby nation's navy will come running to the rescue. Apart from the race having rigid safety regulations, their safety net is within the fleet — their rivals — as was the case in the 1993/94 race. It happened on the leg from Cape Town to Fremantle, a rugged one where the crew of one race yacht reported seeing more than 40 icebergs in a day. The Italian entry, the 60-foot *Brooksfield*, was charging ahead in a gale when, out of the blue, the rudder post ripped out of the bottom of the hull, leaving a hole the size of a basketball. Three tonnes of water belched into the cabin before the crew could begin hand-bailing. Fearing that their yacht was about to sink, the crew radioed an SOS. In 60-knot winds and seas that were like liquid cliffs, the two yachts closest to the drama immediately stopped racing and headed for the crippled *Brooksfield*. The first yacht arrived 12 hours after the SOS went out and stood by in case the crew had to abandon ship.

The *Brooksfield* crew eventually managed to partially plug the gaping hole with a bucket and stem the flow of water to a level at which they could sail themselves, albeit slowly, to Fremantle and safety.

There seems to be some sort of intense magnet that draws the sailors back because a significant number have scaled this Everest three or more times: such as Ross Field, one of the driving forces behind *Team News Corp*. At times, he says, the race experience is like being at the bottom of a ruck in a rugby game getting your head kicked in. 'No one enjoys that. But then things start going your way; you're running with the ball and enjoying it. Suddenly the memory of all the pain disappears and things are worthwhile. You're starting to kick the stuffing out of the opposition.'

After four round-the-world races this 52-year-old Kiwi ex-cop decided he'd had enough of punishing his body so hard for so long. He wanted to stay ashore next time and be sailing's version of Formula One's Frank Williams — a team manager. It started out that way when, along with English sailing associate Jeremy 'Jez' Fanstone, he put together an international team to crew *Team News Corp*. It was all going according to plan until he watched his team come ashore from a couple of practice races. Field knew he was in trouble. The sailing wasn't out of his system . . . he wanted to be out there on the ocean.

Rugged and weatherbeaten with smile lines that crack open like canyons, Field admits there are plenty of times during the race when he wishes he wasn't there. Being home in bed and enjoying eight hours' sleep would be much nicer. But when he gets to the good bits there's no activity on the planet that is more exhilarating. He thrives on the high-velocity, rampaging downwind slides across the Southern Ocean. It's a surfboat ride down the face of monster waves that goes on day after day. It might be blowing 30 knots or more but the spinnaker is set and the boat and crew are under maximum stress. The yacht can surf at better than 25 knots and when the bow wave bursts across the deck and hits you it's like copping the full blast from a fire hose. You hang on, sail as hard as you can, and hope that it all holds together.

Field states that the race is not for amateurs, that there is simply no room for mistakes. 'You have to trust your boat and trust your crew when you're racing down there. The only thing I fear is hitting something at that speed. I often lie in my bunk and say to myself, "Hell, if we hit something now, it isn't going to be pretty." Growlers [low and large blocks of ice the size of a car that wallow on the surface] are an occupational hazard.'

Moments of relaxation and contemplation during the race are rare, although there are plenty of times when crews, especially newcomers, take the time to ask themselves what the hell they are doing out there. Crews must be ever-vigilant and prepared for the prospect of a disaster at any moment. It's like sleeping with one eye open.

The 64-foot hulls are built to be as strong and as light as possible, utilising the latest aerospace technology — a composite construction using Kevlar skins on either side of a foam core. Still, despite the incredible inherent strength of the structure, there is no guarantee that it will survive a high-speed impact with an iceberg, a semi-submerged shipping container or a floating log. Such a collision could see one of these boats bust open like a matchbox being squashed under a size-12 boot.

Stability comes from the pendulum effect of a deep fin keel fitted with a torpedo-shaped lead bulb on its tip, plus 2.5 tonnes of water ballast that can, when required, be pumped into and out of tanks along the windward side of the hull. The power-to-weight ratio on these yachts is critical to performance, a criterion that extends far beyond the yacht itself. The crew must travel as lightly as they can, even down to toothbrush handles being cut in half. What they can take onboard is strictly limited. Forget reading material and cameras for those dreamy sunset shots. Each crewmember survives on meagre rations of around 700 grams of far-from-exciting freeze-dried food per day. Combine this meagre diet and the energy expended and you get a weight loss program that really works. On the longer legs, which can take up to a month, some crewmembers can lose 10 kilograms or more. Even drinking water is considered a weighty luxury. It comes via a water-maker attached to the yacht's engine.

Crews can forget about a rest if they are too tired to continue. There are no fresh run-on reserves on the sidelines waiting to take their place. Sleep deprivation is a fact of life and depression is common. So is seasickness. And while these boats are among the most sophisticated rocket ships imaginable, they are hell ships when it comes to creature comforts, both on deck and below. Automatic pilots are not permitted; sails are constantly trimmed to every whim of wind and wave. Weight distribution — windward, leeward, forward or aft — is critical to the yacht's speed, so with every change in direction there is a flurry of activity below deck. Everything has to be moved to the high side — sails, personal equipment, bunks and even the stove. Then, when it comes to a tack or gybe and the wind is on the other side, the entire procedure is repeated in reverse. The off-watch trying to catch some shut-eye become the furniture removalists, hauling themselves from their bunks, shifting everything, then climbing back into the bunks on the new high side. If sails need changing or there's a drama on deck, they can cancel any hope of sleep.

'Home', such as it is, is forever moving, rocking, rolling, slamming, and pounding. When things are rough, everything is wet: bunks, sleeping bags, and clothes, all icy cold in the Southern Ocean. Water sloshes around your feet inside the cabin, and the wetter it gets, the more it stinks. It's rancid down there. Twelve bodies must exist below deck in an area the size of a small kitchen. This space is your bedroom, bathroom, living room, sauna and navigation station all crammed into one. It's like a rabbit warren. Showers? No way. Full ablution opportunities only come when a rain shower passes overhead, and that's only when it's warm enough. When it's bitterly cold the last thing you want to do is shed the warmth of your thermal clothing and survival suit. And as for a change of clothing, well, crews joke that you turn your underpants inside out after two weeks.

The track for the 2001/2002 race was to be the longest and most arduous ever. It took the fleet from the start in England to Cape Town, Sydney, and Auckland via Hobart, Rio de Janeiro, Miami, Baltimore/Annapolis on the US east coast, France's La Rochelle, Sweden's Gothenburg and, finally, Kiel in Germany. It would test eight of the best crews in the world to the absolute limit.

LEG	START/RESTART	DEPART	STOPOVER	NM
1	Southampton	23/09/2001	Cape Town	7350
2	Cape Town	11/11/2001	Sydney	6550
3	Sydney (via Hobart)	26/12/2001	Auckland	2050
4	Auckland	27/01/2002	Rio de Janeiro	6700
5	Rio de Janeiro	09/03/2002	Miami	4450
6	Miami	14/04/2002	Baltimore	875
7	Annapolis	28/04/2002	La Rochelle	3400
8	La Rochelle	25/05/2002	Gothenburg	1075
9	Gothenburg	08/06/2002	Kiel	250

THE LAUNCHING PAD

This is one of the toughest sports there is in the world.

**KAY COTTEE AO — THE FIRST WOMAN TO SAIL SOLO,
NONSTOP AND UNASSISTED AROUND THE WORLD**

the securing of sponsorship for a racing yacht in a major international yachting event like the Volvo Ocean Race is rarely easy. High-profile spectator sports such as motor racing and football create the highest hurdles for sailors. Ross Field and Jez Fanstone, like most other potential competitors, had been knocking on corporate doors around the world in their bid to dig up the dollars for a VOR campaign. When it came time to visit News Corp, via an introduction through a sailing associate, it was a classic case of being in the right place at the right time.

For these would-be ocean warriors it was a rather circuitous route that took them to News Corporation's Rupert and Lachlan Murdoch.

The initial introduction to Lachlan came through Frenchman Oli Allard, a 35-year-old one-time professional golfer who had switched careers to his other great love, sailing. Oli met Lachlan after moving to Sydney and being invited to join the crew of Lachlan's cruising/racing yacht, *Karakoram*. Oli had also sailed with Jez aboard a similar-style race yacht at regattas in Australia's tropical north a few years previously. This all led to Jez, Ross and Oli travelling to New York to present their round-the-world race proposal to Lachlan.

One aspect of the proposal for this global event the Murdochs seized on was the excellent opportunity for a staff incentive program to be built linking all divisions worldwide. While News Corp was not a market brandname as such, it was the umbrella covering more than 35 000 employees.

With the presentation complete in New York, Ross and Jez decided they should return to Jez's home in England and wait to hear if they'd been successful.

A FEW WEEKS later, Jez was in his garden trimming a hedge while Ross, a far-from-avid gardener, was inside keeping his mind active by playing solitaire on his computer. The first sign for Jez that something unusual was brewing was the way Ross came rushing around the back of the house with his trademark grin almost doing a lap of honour around his face. He looked like the cat who had just got the canary. 'We've got the money,' he shouted exuberantly. 'Lachlan's just called. They're going to go with us!' He couldn't stop grinning.

Jez, known for talking in slow motion, mustered every ounce of excitement available to him: 'Shit, that's fantastic,' was his response. It was accompanied by a look of stunned disbelief, for he had just gone from casually trimming a hedge to being the skipper of a round-the-world racer. All the dreams he had harboured since first reading a book about the Whitbread Race as a 10-year-old in England were about to come true. He knew back then that he wanted to lead a crew when he was a 'grown-up'. His next reaction was: 'Hell, have we got some work to do now!' Planning would have to start immediately.

Not surprisingly, Oli Allard was the first team appointment — he would be the shore-based yacht maintenance manager, the boss of the pit crew.

From News Corp's perspective the race became the inspiration for the company's first global employee recognition program, rewarding valued employees with trips to watch the race starts and to meet and sail with the crew in various ports around the world. It also represented a tremendous marketing and communications opportunity for other divisions — including *The Daily Telegraph* newspaper in Australia, *The Times* in London, and National Geographic Channel International.

It was the first time they had done anything like it on an international scale, according to vice-president of marketing at News Corp, Spencer Moseska. 'It wasn't that it had never been considered, it's just that we'd never found an external vehicle that would be relevant — and even inspiring — to our employees worldwide. The Volvo Ocean Race was the ideal way to unite, excite, and motivate our employees.'

Staff were excited about the incentive program before the race started. More than 1000 employees were at the launching of the yacht at New York's Chelsea Pier. It was called *Team News Corp*.

Ross and Jez went to the Volvo race office thrilled that Lachlan had called and said News Corp would be their sponsor. 'We met with one of the officials, announced with great pride that we had our money and were ready to break out the champagne,' says Ross. 'His only response was, "Oh, with News Corp. We may not accept your entry." Instead of being enthusiastic about a confirmed entry, his reaction was that the race media program might be hijacked.'

In the end the officials realised the value of having News Corp associated with the race — that there would be no threat to the race, only benefits.

_/2_

THE FIRST TICK of the second hand on the project came about because of sailor Leah Newbold, and her relationship with Jez. Leah, who had the two previous round-the-world races behind her as a member of all-women crews, had met Jez in Cape Town during the 1997/98 race. Their blossoming relationship meant that they spent considerable time in Auckland, where Leah shared a house with her close friend, Ross Field, who she describes as being the next best thing to a brother.

Jez had started sailing at the age of eight with his father in a Mirror dinghy in England. His talents saw him selected to the UK youth sailing squad but, while at university studying for a degree in philosophy and sociology, sailing took a back seat. The sport reclaimed him later, so much so that instead of following the career path the university degree offered, he became a sailmaker and yacht builder.

With the 1997/98 round-the-world race completed and his relationship with Leah developing, Jez began thinking the unthinkable: that it might be time to 'get a real job'. He was rescued from this fate when he and Ross started talking about the possibility of creating a campaign for the 2001/2002 race: 'I liked Jez straight away,' says Ross, 'because he seemed to have the same sort of attitude towards sailing as I did. One day I just said to him: "Why don't you pull your finger out and put a campaign together and I'll give you a hand?" He grabbed the idea and off we went.'

In association with British-based banker Eddie Charlton, Ross and Jez set up a company, Ocean Sports Management, with the sole purpose, initially, of securing funding for a Volvo Ocean Race campaign. Within Ocean Sports Management Ross would be the campaign manager and Jez the skipper for the VOR. Jez also created another partnership in February 2001 when he and Leah were married. There was a bonus for the campaign as a result of this union — the syndicate gained an experienced shore manager in Leah, who had decided after the last race that she had had enough of competing. She had done it twice and not done well twice, she says. 'It was particularly frustrating after the last one where we had everything needed to win — the yacht and equipment — but still couldn't be competitive. It's extremely difficult for women in a race like this because they are nowhere near as strong as the guys. It shows when things get tough, like handling the big sails in strong winds. There's also a lack of women with the experience needed to be competitive. They might be great sailors in their own right, but sailing around the world is very different to anything else. I think the final crunch came for me when we were dismasted halfway between New Zealand and Cape Horn the last time. The 11 days it took to sail under a jury rig to a port at the tip of Cape Horn were probably the worst days of my life. I knew it was all over for me when I was saying to myself, "I can do without this. Why am I putting my life at risk?"'

Leah's job description was to make sure that everything ran smoothly for the *News Corp* team when they were ashore: she would run all the administration and logistics for the team and the boat, including freight, travel and accommodation. 'I guess my real job is to make sure that life's as easy as possible for the crew when they're in port. If they want a fitting for the boat I have to find it and get it delivered. I also have to look after the transport of the shipping containers that we leapfrog from port to port. They are our mobile workshops,' she says.

The initial News Corp 'management family' became more complete when Ross's partner, Jan van der Lee, was included as nutritional coordinator. It was a logical move, considering her background in nutrition, fitness and natural therapies. Also, having travelled with Ross during the previous race, she knew what would be needed. Still, that didn't make it any easier to make more palatable the freeze-dried food they would eat during the entire voyage. That was a real challenge.

Another early recruit was Ashley Abbott, a 30-year-old languages and politics graduate from universities in Auckland and Tokyo, who was signed on as PR and communications manager.

WITH KIWIS FORMING the core of the team and News Corp deciding that the entry would be the first ever to race under the Australian flag — representing Sydney's Cruising Yacht Club of Australia — it wasn't difficult for Ross and Jez to decide to base themselves in the Antipodes. By having the campaign headquarters in Auckland, they had access to some of the world's best boat builders, rig manufacturers and sailmakers. They could also train during the southern hemisphere summer and have much easier access to the 2000 Sydney to Hobart race. That 630-mile race was a much-desired segment of the training program as it was to be part of the third stage of the Volvo Ocean Race the following year. They would, in fact, sail the entire course for Leg Three by continuing onto Auckland after reaching Hobart.

Another easy decision was the choice of designer for the race yacht. Ross and Jez enlisted expatriate New Zealander Bruce Farr, now based in Annapolis on the east coast of the United States, who had designed more winners of this race than anyone else. And the Cookson yard in Auckland got the job of building the boat.

The construction phase turned out to be an interesting experience. The Cookson yard was building another Volvo race yacht, the Norwegian entry *djuice dragons*, so there was an element of secrecy at the site. *djuice* had been designed by another Kiwi, Laurie Davidson, and was quite different to the Farr breed of VO 60s, as the class is known. Mid-construction there were accusations of espionage from the rival camp, all based on the fact that one day at lunchtime Jez, while innocently eating a steak and onion pie, happened to walk past the shed where *djuice* was being built. The large doors at the entrance to the shed were wide open so, not surprisingly, Jez turned his attention from the contents of the pie to the stern of the yacht that was clearly visible. 'Spy, spy!' was the gist of a fax from the *djuice* team to the *Team News Corp* camp. 'If it's such a secret then keep your doors shut,' was the terse response.

By mid-December 2000 the entire *News Corp* team was in Sydney preparing the recently purchased VO 60 training yacht for the Sydney to Hobart race. Everything was running smoothly until Ross pulled Jez aside one morning and quietly said to him, 'The shit's hit the fan.' He had just spoken with the boat builder, Mick Cookson, in Auckland. Three weeks into the building process it had been discovered that on a significant area of the hull the outer and inner Kevlar skins had not bonded to the internal foam core; without the bond, there was no inherent strength in the hull. It was a disaster.

Ross flew to Auckland immediately where, after seeing the extent of the problem, he decided that there was only one solution: to trash the hull and start again. Returning to Sydney to keep the crew's focus on the Sydney to Hobart race, he also had to make them very aware that their project was now a very precious month behind schedule. They would all have to work even harder.

It was the 56th staging of the annual Sydney to Hobart yacht race, and on the morning of the start the Cruising Yacht Club's dock was something akin to organised chaos. There was a particular crush around the *Team News Corp* training yacht, primarily because Lachlan Murdoch, who was part of the crew for the race, and his beautiful wife, Sarah O'Hare, had arrived. The paparazzi crowded around, pressing for pictures of the high-profile pair, then Rupert Murdoch and his wife, Wendi, arrived to wish the team well so another media scrum ensued. In the middle of it all was the always-energetic PR manager, Ashley Abbott, who is known for her love of pets. She was immediately attracted to Sarah's small dog, Grace, which she bent down to pat. At that moment someone on the yacht distracted her attention. When she returned her gaze to the dog it wasn't Grace that she was patting; she was fondling Rupert Murdoch's leg! He either didn't notice or didn't care.

The fleet set sail from Sydney's magnificent harbour on a gloriously sunny day. Thousands of spectator craft escorted the yachts to the open sea while tens of thousands lined the shore, soaking up the excitement of what is an iconic Australian summer sporting fixture. Three other VOR syndicates were using the race and the sprint to Auckland as part of their training program for the main event.

Team News Corp led its rivals through the entrance to Sydney Harbour but the period of glory was brief. The race result was a bitter disappointment as the crew were faced with problems from start to finish. They trailed two other VOR teams, *illbruck* (John Kostecki) and *Tyco* (Kevin

Shoebridge) home by nearly five hours, a significant margin considering it was only a three-day race.

Equally disappointing was the result of the match-up the VO 60s then had from Hobart to Auckland. It was blatantly obvious that *Team News Corp* was a long way from being competitive for the race around the planet due to start just nine months later. Three days after arriving in Auckland the consequences of the Sydney to Hobart exercise affected the team like an earth tremor — there were resignations and dismissals — but Ross and Jez were not concerned. They knew that this was all part of the team-building process and race preparation.

There was, however, a positive sign emerging for the team. Ross was becoming increasingly aware that the excitement this type of ocean racing brings was still running strongly through his veins — he wanted to be part of the Volvo Ocean Race. He and Jez talked about it; there was no doubt that his experience would bring invaluable strength to the team. So, once again, Ross took his sea boots off the hook to become the tactical navigator.

By the race start date, 23 September 2001, *Team News Corp* would boast one of the best crews in the world, and it would get better. The team was an impressive blend of sailors with long-distance racing experience, youthful determination, tactical efficiency and meteorological knowledge.

WHILE THE RACE boat was being built in Auckland the team continued their intense program of sail development and crew training, both on and off the water. Confidence and enthusiasm was mounting. One major asset for the team was the inclusion of New Zealander Jeff Scott, a passionate sailor and fisherman. He started his round-the-world racing career in the 1989/90 Whitbread Race and was with Ross four years later when they won, sailing *Yamaha*. A man of few words, Jeff was to be watch leader in the 12-person crew. Highly experienced Australian sailmaker Alby Pratt also joined the team, as did Jon 'Gundy' Gunderson, a good sailor as much as the provider of solid humour, even when the going was tough. Nick White, a respected sailing meteorologist, became the man who would be onboard looking into the crystal ball for weather guidance.

There was more good news in mid-February: construction of the new boat was five days ahead of schedule. Valuable preparation time lost with the scrapping of the first hull was being regained.

AS THE HULL neared completion there was an interesting decision from within the News Corp organisation. To create effective 'branding', the marketers decided that one name could unite the campaign and the crew worldwide and become a team mascot. Aged 10, full of mischief, and a resident of Springfield, Bart Simpson was chosen, and he would become the best-known face in the race.

News Corp representatives and the yacht crew were looking for a paint design for the boat that would give the hull a lift, and provide an atmosphere of fun that would appeal to a wide range of people. Conventional designs were just that, conventional. Before they knew it, Bart's head had bobbed up. With him being part of the News Corp entertainment family, it was an easy choice.

Los Angeles-based Julius Preitus, an animator with Fox and one of the few people in the world qualified and authorised to draw *Simpsons* characters, came up with the image of Bart Simpson urging the boat onwards. That image was to feature on each side of the hull near the stern. Bart's head also dominated the largest of *Team News Corp*'s spinnakers.

AFTER MORE THAN 20 000 working hours and the use of two tonnes of resin plus hundreds of metres of Kevlar cloth, by mid-May the new race boat was completed and ready to go. When it emerged from Cookson's shed to be launched and rigged, keen observers noted that the hull was not as bright and shiny as one would expect of a new yacht. There was good reason for this. In finishing the hull with a flat undercoat and not gloss paint, the surface would be smoother, which is better for speed, and there would be an associated weight-saving by not applying the gloss paint needed to cover a hull 64 feet long.

The first outing for *Team News Corp* was a 500-mile coastal dash in winds that gusted to 30 knots and nasty seas — just the conditions the crew wanted. The boat came back to the dock with the usual large number of little problems to be fixed, but overall its potential was clear.

Four weeks later it was time to pack up the Auckland base. Much of the equipment was to be sent to Southampton in the UK for the start, while the yacht was to be shipped to New York for its naming ceremony and four weeks of corporate-hospitality sailing. This would be followed by a practice race across the Atlantic to England with two Volvo Ocean Race rivals.

$$\Delta$$

BY THE TIME it reached New York, *Team News Corp* was already battle-scarred, and it hadn't even raced. First, the tip of the wing-like rudder was knocked off in Auckland when an unobservant motorist drove into it while the yacht was sitting in its cradle onshore. Next, the deck was damaged when the jib of the crane hit the boat while it was being lifted onto the ship. Then, when the yacht arrived in the Big Apple it was more black than blue and white in colour — thanks to its proximity on deck to the ship's smoke-belching funnel during the voyage.

The cleaning process before launching in New York was easy compared with the problem discovered in the hull: delamination — the curse of composite-built boats. One area of the hull on the starboard (right-hand) side aft had bubbled. Technically it's called 'gassing', which is usually the result of the foam sheets used as the core between the outer and inner Kevlar skins not being processed properly. During manufacturing the foam sheets go through a process that should remove all excess gases from the material. It appeared that at least one of the sheets used for *Team News Corp* was a bad egg. Ross and Jez debated the problem with the foam manufacturer and Cookson's sent a specialist boat builder to New York to fix it. He used a vacuum procedure to literally suck the bubbled areas back onto the foam.

The corporate-hospitality sailing in New York for News Corp staff and major clients was remarkably well received and had the desired impact. There were lots of laughs for both crew and guests. For many guests the invitation to go sailing on the Hudson River had them convinced that they would be boarding one of the multi-million-dollar mega yachts they could see dominating the scene when they arrived at the marina. How wrong they were. There were looks of astonishment and polite comments of 'Oh … this is it', when they were escorted down the dock to yachting's equivalent of a Formula One race car — a purpose-built, stripped-out and streamlined ocean racer. But at the end of each outing the guests were thrilled. The excitement of sailing on a purebred racing yacht, plus their appreciation of the project, confirmed that *Team News Corp* was an extremely valuable promotional tool. The guests struggled, however, to appreciate the lack of creature comforts below deck. 'You cook on that thing for 12 people?' inquired one woman, pointing at the tiny single burner stove that would barely be suitable for camping.

'Yeah, you don't go on this race for the food,' Gundy assured her.

The toilet, a basic white plastic bowl immediately adjacent to the stove and without any privacy screen, was another high point of conversation.

At the launch party at Chelsea Pier, Fox Television presenter Paula Zahn joined Rupert Murdoch on the bow of the yacht and smashed the champagne, then the crew turned on a sailing display metres from the dock that brought gasps, cheers and applause from the colourful crowd. Two days later *Team News Corp* would be racing across the Atlantic against two of the favourites for the Volvo Ocean Race, *Team Tyco* and *illbruck Challenge*, in what was another build-up to the start.

THE SEPTEMBER 11 terrorist attacks on the World Trade Centre had a particular impact on the emotions of the *News Corp* crew. In New York just a few weeks earlier their lives had revolved around the World Trade Centre, its vibrant and always busy shopping malls, restaurants and bars. They had stayed at a hotel adjacent to the towers and the yacht was docked at the centre's North Cove Marina.

Their thoughts after September 11 were with the thousands of workers they had seen coming off the ferries each morning, walking past them at the dock and streaming into the towers to begin a day's work. How many of those innocent people had survived?

Top News Corp staff gather in New York to toast the success of *Team News Corp* at its official launch.

Centre After being named, *Team News Corp* does a sailpast for staff at New York's Chelsea Pier.

Bottom At the helm. Rupert Murdoch steers *Team News Corp* on New York's Hudson River while Ross Field (*third from left*) looks on.

All images *Richard Langdon/Ocean Images*

THE COUNTDOWN

We all knew that if he didn't do the first leg

he wouldn't do any of the race because he would just go home

and find it very hard to recover.

**JEZ FANSTONE ON NICK WHITE FOLLOWING THE DEATH
OF NICK'S PARTNER, FIONA SALKELD**

as much as the team enjoyed being in New York they were equally happy to be at sea, crossing the Atlantic in full racing mode. This was the first time their new charge had lined up against any of the opposition; and fortunately this was good opposition. Both John Kostecki's *illbruck* and Kevin Shoebridge's *Tyco* were known to have the ability to win the Volvo Ocean Race. Would *Team News Corp* be on the pace? Had they got the formula right or would they need to make wholesale changes to the yacht and team once they had crossed the puddle and reached England? There was also the realisation of just how 'friendly' it is racing in the claustrophobic confines of a VO 60-class yacht. This was excellent training just weeks before the looming start date of 23 September.

Two-time America's Cup-winning navigator Peter Isler had agreed to sail with *Team News Corp* for the shorter legs of the Volvo Ocean Race. He joined the crew for the 2800-nautical mile crossing of the Atlantic so he could get the feel for how things operated. This crossing would be an invaluable experience because, despite this being an informal clash, the race mode on the yacht extended right through to team progress reports being sent via email back to shore daily, just as would be required of all crews in the VOR.

The Atlantic trip officially qualified the yacht for the VOR. It also tested the structure, rig, crew and equipment in conditions ranging from zero wind and flat seas to 35 knots and very rough ocean conditions.

The crossing was a tough test, according to Jez: 'We lost a sail and had technical problems with our generator, but I was very happy with our performance. Having Peter there brought a fresh look at our systems, our technical gear and how we make our decisions.'

Ross's take on the trip was that both good and bad decisions were made by all the boats, but at the end of the 11 days they all finished very close together. 'The Volvo Ocean Race is made up of nine races, like the Formula One Grand Prix. With eight well-prepared teams with very similar boats, it's going to be close.'

The pre-race odds for the Volvo Ocean Race had *Team News Corp* ranked by the yachting media a fifth-favourite outsider at 9–1, with *illbruck* considered the boat to beat at 5–1. Influencing the theory behind *Team*

News Corp's ranking was that they were a one-boat campaign; they had not enhanced their race preparations by building two boats for more effective sail, hull and crew evaluation. The favouritism towards *illbruck* was justified, as they were the first team to nominate for the race and had therefore enjoyed the benefit of more time to develop the hull, sail inventory and crew. But the odds makers had a rethink about the Australian entry when just six weeks before the start they showed the way home to three other VOR racers contesting the gruelling Fastnet Race out of England. It started in Cowes, went via Fastnet Rock off Ireland and finished in Plymouth. *illbruck*, which was placed second to *Team News Corp* in the Fastnet Race, remained the favourite for the VOR, but it was nice for the *News Corp* team to win the final shakedown.

_____/)____

THE FOCUS MOVED to Southampton, where the fleet of eight great yachts and, equally, eight top-shelf crews, assembled for the 23 September kick-off. Special dispensation was given to the all-female crew sailing *Amer Sports Too* (skippered by Lisa McDonald) to carry 13 crew instead of 12. This was done for safety reasons.

Six of the eight yachts were the product of the Bruce Farr design office in America. Along with *Team News Corp*, these were *illbruck*, *Tyco*, *Amer Sports Too*, *Team SEB* and *ASSA ABLOY*. New Zealander Laurie Davidson designed *djuice dragons*, while *Amer Sports One* was designed by Italian-based Mani Frers. On paper the fleet looked remarkably equal in terms of design, talent and funding. Most of the sponsors were based in Europe and were using the Volvo Ocean Race to promote their exceptionally large organisations to the world. Like Formula One motor racing, this competition is about sponsors and not nations. The skippers and crews were drawn from around the world. The starters and riders read this way:

ASSA ABLOY (Sweden) Skipper: Roy Heiner (Netherlands)
Amer Sports One (Italy) Skipper: Grant Dalton (New Zealand)

Amer Sports Too (Italy) Skipper: Lisa McDonald (USA)

djuice dragons (Norway) Skipper: Knut Frostad (Norway)

illbruck Challenge (Germany) Skipper: John Kostecki (USA)

Team News Corp (Australia) Skipper: Jez Fanstone (UK)

Team SEB (Sweden) Skipper: Gunnar 'Gurra' Krantz (Sweden)

Team Tyco (Bermuda) Skipper: Kevin Shoebridge (New Zealand)

SAVING WEIGHT WAS crucial. The basic theory is that the lighter the boat, the faster it goes. Everything was under scrutiny, including the food taken onboard. Team nutritionist Jan van der Lee had a difficult job: to provide the minimum amount of food offering the most amount of nutrition. Her job was made even more difficult by the fact that she also had to make freeze-dried food interesting enough to keep the crew happy. It was very much a case of making a silk purse out of a sow's ear.

She worked closely with a dietician in Auckland formulating the freeze-dried food menus. She then ordered the food, along with all the other necessary items, such as toilet rolls, and vacuum-packed it all, even the toilet rolls, so they stayed dry and took up minimum space.

Jan explains how it's done: 'We do it by days. You start with day zero when we provide fresh food. Then from day one they're into full freeze-dried food for breakfast, lunch and dinner. There are three meals and four snacks over a period of 24 hours. Breakfast is muesli or some kind of cereal, protein powder and milk powder crackers. Protein powder, which you mix with water like a shake, is a combination of carbohydrate and protein. If they're not getting enough calories they start burning lean muscle mass. That's where you start getting into problems and they really start losing weight.

'The weight allocation is 18 kilograms for two days, which works out at around 700 grams of food per person per day. They are getting about 5000 calories a day. Usually, doing the work that they are doing, they would need 6000 to 7000 calories per day, but it's very hard to get the amount of calories in 700 grams of food, and for it to have some nutritional value as well.

'Everything revolves around food being cooked using water. We try to give them variation: Thai chicken curry, chilli con carne, lamb fettuccine, roast chicken and lamb, beef stroganoff and some fish dishes with parsley sauce. But the meals are nowhere as exciting as they might sound. For example, the meat used looks more like kebab meat or reconstituted meat.'

LESS THAN THREE weeks before the race start a devastating tragedy hit the team. Onboard meteorologist Nick White's 28-year-old partner, Fiona Salkeld, suddenly collapsed and died one night while staying with Nick at the crew house in Southampton. She had suffered heart failure. A heavy cloud of shock and grief descended over the entire crew. Fiona was considered part of the team — she had planned to travel to every port to be with Nick. In addition to their emotional burden, Jez and Ross had to contend with the fact that one of the key crew members, the man charged with maintaining all their computers and communications links, plus expert analysis of weather patterns, would now probably drop out of the race.

Jez Fanstone:

> Ross and I had a lot of thinking to do. As a precaution, we had to plan for a replacement. It was too early for Nick to even consider whether or not he would be staying with us, but we had to address the problem. The following day we were talking about the options we had available at such short notice. I thought about it and decided that at the end of the day, in a purely selfish world, Nick was the best person for the boat. None of the other people Ross and I considered came close to what we had in Nick.
>
> The two of us also had to plan what we could do to help Nick in this terrible situation. We sat him down to talk him through everything. I decided it was best to take it from the top. I said to him: 'Look, Nick, from a selfish

point of view, you must be on the boat with us. At the same time we believe that being on the boat will help you. The plan is that Ross will fly back with you to New Zealand, be with you the whole time, help organise the funeral and everything else that has to be sorted out. He has contacts across New Zealand and can take a big load off your mind.'

We were pleased to see Nick was actually quite relieved when we sat him down. He was very grateful that we'd thought things through for him and that Ross was going to go back to New Zealand. Nick doesn't like imposing on people; you find that in his work, especially working on the boat. He won't tell you he has a problem; he won't tell you he has too much work. We almost forced him into doing something by saying, 'Right, here's the plan. We are going to go back and sort you out; we are going to bring you back and get you on the boat. You're going to do the first leg because you're the person we want.' He could very easily have turned around and said, 'Stick it up your arse,' but he obviously knew it was the right thing to do. For a week he was very low. He and I talked at length at the time. It was very hard for him to break through that, but he did. We all knew that if he didn't do the first leg he wouldn't do any of the race because he would just go home and find it very hard to recover. By sailing with us he had something to focus on.

Ross arrived back in Southampton with Nick just days before the start to find everything going according to plan. *Team News Corp* was ready to race around the planet.

Top The skippers and navigators at the pre-race media conference.
Centre Race veteran Ross Field farewells his partner, Jan van der Lee, in Southampton.
Bottom The fleet lines up before the start in Southampton.

All images *Richard Langdon/Ocean Images*

≫ SOUTHAMPTON TO CAPE TOWN

We went up this huge wave ... there was nothing behind it

except air. It was like driving a car over a cliff ... I've no

doubt that the only thing still in the water was the tip of

the rudder ... even the keel and bulb were completely out of the

water. The crash ... was like landing on concrete.

ROSS FIELD

the atmosphere on lift-off day for the Volvo Ocean Race was like the final stage of countdown before a space shuttle launch. An air of eager anticipation prevailed.

After 18 months of planning and preparation, Jez and his crew were ready to go. They had a big breakfast, their last decent meal, before heading down to the boat armed with minimum personal needs for their next month at sea — a toothbrush, a pair of thermals, a T-shirt, a pair of shorts, a pair of boxers, a midlayer jacket, a beanie and a sunhat. That was it — no books, spare clothes or even soap!

There was only one thing on the crew's mind: 'Let's get out of here!' After such an intense build-up for their nine-month odyssey it was time to go racing.

Ross Field:

I think we're in good shape. We definitely have the ability to win; but it's never far from our mind that this is a nine-leg race or, more specifically, a nine-race event. Guys have won gold medals at the Olympics without even winning a race, so we might go through the whole thing without winning a leg. But as long as we're consistent we will win the race. We just have to plug away at the target — we don't need to be radical in any department unless we totally believe that it's the right way to go.

Compared with some other teams, theirs was a low-key departure from the dock. That was how they wanted it. Family, partners and friends gathered for a final farewell. There were hugs, waves, smiles, lots of kisses and a few tears as the docklines were dropped and the blue and white yacht glided away towards the Solent. The team's chosen battle song, Apollo Four Forty's 'Stop the Rock', belted out at maximum decibels in the background. Special thoughts went out to Nick, who was obviously feeling a level of remoteness from the scene.

At 3pm on 23 September, HRH Prince Andrew fired a cannon from the deck of a large ship moored on the Solent off Cowes to signal the start of the 7350-mile leg to Cape Town. Brightness was brought to an otherwise grey day by the hundreds of spectator craft — launches, yachts, small inflatables, dinghies, and even canoes — escorting the eight race boats on a course towards the open sea. Helicopters droned overhead like giant dragonflies, the television cameramen and photographers aboard them straining for the best possible pictures.

Amer Sports One (Grant Dalton) led the fleet out of the Solent with *Team News Corp* third behind *djuice dragons*. Now aiming into the Atlantic, the yachts were beginning to buck and pitch — perpetual motion for a month, all the way to Cape Town.

Ross Field:

I told the guys I wanted to get over the start line cleanly and not get involved in any situation that might lead to a penalty. We achieved that, but we made the mistake of setting a sail for what we thought the wind would do, not what the wind was doing at the time. We expected it to move more behind us, but it didn't.

Probably the most memorable moment was right after we all cleared the fairway buoy and lined up for the first time. With a spinnaker on we sailed over the top of illbruck *and* Tyco *like there was no tomorrow. That gave us a little bit of encouragement — like, we really were in the hunt. After that we found that every time we lost some miles we could always hang in there and get them back. For me it was a very good sign that the boat was on the pace; that we had the ability to recover. We knew right then we had a boat that could do the job; that with the inevitable modifications and revamping, we could pull it off.*

Alby Pratt:

Everyone aboard Team News Corp *was stoked to be finally on our way and racing after such a long build-up. All the guys who were saying sad goodbyes to wives and*

*girlfriends just three hours ago now have huge grins on
their faces. The realisation has hit them that this is what
we had come for, that there's no more boat work, no
more sail work, no more food to pack; all we now had to
do was to race.*

For the month it would take to complete this leg (and for the entire course around the globe) the race could be followed by enthusiasts as though they were ringside. The media coverage was the most technologically advanced ever, with each crew sending back daily emails, still photographs, video footage and satellite phone messages relating to life onboard. Beyond that, the Virtual Spectator computer program provided a visual assessment of what was happening out on the water. Using data gathered from each yacht at regular intervals — latitude, longitude, course, wind speed, boat speed, wave height, etc — computer graphics were generated and put into real life situations. You could log on and literally see how the race was unfolding, what tactics were being applied and when the yachts were expected to finish. It was compulsory viewing for the world's armchair admirals.

BASED ON WORLD weather patterns the course for this race is primarily downwind; the yachts follow much the same global wind systems that propelled sailing ships around the world from west to east centuries ago. Certainly for this first leg, delightfully fast downwind sailing was expected for the majority of the time. Expected, yes, but in reality this time, wrong!

Ross:
*You never expect a good bash upwind after the start out
of England, but that's what we're getting. It's tough
going because we're trying to adjust from city life and
we're being thrown in at the deep end, bashing and*

crashing uphill. It's a big adjustment — no one's been eating. The only thing going through everyone's mind when it's like this is, 'Why the stuff am I doing this when I could be at home in a nice double bed, curled up in clean sheets? Here I am, bashing my guts out and not enjoying it.' In short, the Bay of Biscay is bloody terrible. I'm thinking we are in the wrong race. It feels like we're in the race that goes around the world against the wind. It's on the nose and blowing hard: 25 to 30 knots, but the consolation is that we are fast when we are sailing upwind.

The rough weather was a brutal awakening for all crews to the facts of life in this elite level of ocean racing. It was as though they'd stepped off a cliff without having time to look over the edge.

Gundy (Jon Gunderson):

I've just been informed that I have to get back on deck for another watch. I honestly thought that I had just come down here … four hours can go fast! The weather invariably makes my job quite a lot harder; food becomes harder to cook with the angle and bouncing around — finding motivation to set up cameras, take photos and sit here in the media station, getting it all together, is difficult.

… We are all still trying to get fully settled in. It's hard to sleep during the day and hard to stay awake at night. Right now I am starting to get a little queasy trying to type on this thing, so I'm outta here!

Seasickness was rife across the fleet as crewmembers struggled to find their sea legs, and with the seasickness came lack of sleep. But all crews pushed as hard as they could, none better than *illbruck* which had managed to pass *Tyco* and lead the race south.

Team News Corp was positioned to the west of the fleet and very much in touch with the lead when the first onboard drama arrived. Damian 'Shreda' Duke, the most recent recruit to the crew, was down below when the yacht launched itself off a particularly nasty wave and crashed into the trough that followed. It was like accelerating into a brick wall in a car — he became a human missile, launched across the cabin at what would prove to be a blistering pace.

Shreda:

It was 8am. I was putting on my wet-weather gear while trying to munch on my porridge at the same time. The boat came off a very big wave and I lost my grip. I went flying across the cabin and in doing so managed to take out the stove and kettle — which was boiling. Worse still, my bowl of porridge was upended in the bilge. The boiling water had gone down my back and was burning my bum through the thermals I was wearing; but I was more worried about my porridge. I was just standing there staring in the bilge, totally distressed, saying, 'That's my porridge. That's my breakfast.'

As I started to scoop the porridge out of the bilge and plop it back into the bowl I realised the boiling water had done some serious damage to my bum. It was really starting to hurt. Realising I was in pain, Smiley [Craig Smith] leapt out of his bunk with the intention of spraying salt water on the burn. I told him to bugger off, because I didn't want to have my thermals caked in salt for the rest of the trip. Alby, the crew medic, came to the rescue. He had the pleasure of applying burn cream to the blisters on my bum for the next week. I'd have to bend over one of the bunks and he'd apply the cream — great dedication on his part. The only real problem was that for the first few days I couldn't sit down when I was on deck, and when I was in my bunk I had to lie on my stomach.

Most importantly, though, I got to finish my porridge,
complete with whatever came out of the bilge with it.

After five days of punishment sailing across the Bay of Biscay north of
Spain and deeper towards the equator, the weather began to improve. The
sea surface became smoother and spinnakers were set in conditions that just
about everyone preferred. *Team News Corp* had been slowed slightly by
equipment failures and a torn spinnaker, but they were still there with the
leaders. The busiest man on the boat was sailmaker Alby Pratt, who had a
24-hour work schedule ahead of him repairing the Code 3 spinnaker that
had exploded. He was crouched on the cabin floor using a portable sewing
machine, trying to match up the pieces and replace the bits that weren't
there.

Code numbers identify the spinnakers and headsails on a VO 60, and the
higher the numeral, the stronger the wind range in which the sail can be
used. If the wind suddenly increases in strength and goes beyond the design
limit of a sail, it will almost certainly blow out. The challenge for the crews
was to get the sail down before this happened and replace it with one suited
to the new conditions.

All seven other yachts were also being tested. The problem *Team SEB*
were experiencing was more serious than a blown-out sail. The metal fitting
at the top of the mainsail (headboard car) that attaches the sail to the mast
had failed. The only option was to change course to the west and head for
the small island of Porto Santo, 60 miles north-east of Madeira, to collect a
spare. (The VOR rules permit outside assistance under clearly defined
circumstances.) The replacement had to be flown to the island from Sweden
and taken offshore on a deep-sea fishing boat chartered to rendezvous with
the yacht.

It was a similar story aboard *djuice dragons*, where a near-identical
headboard car also failed. The crew had lashed the mainsail to the masthead
to keep it aloft, but as watch leader Espen Guttormsen explained, it was a
remedy that complicated things: 'The wind is increasing and we are
wondering how to reef this mainsail, which is lashed to the top of the mast.
The only way to reef it is to send someone up the rig to cut the lashing.

I don't think there are too many volunteers to go up that rig in these conditions. He would break something for sure (himself — not the rig!).'

djuice's skipper, Knut Frostad, decided they would make a pitstop to pick up spare parts at Fernando de Noronha, an island off the Brazilian coast, around 2000 miles ahead. The VOR fleet would be rounding this dot in the middle of the Atlantic as a mark of the course to Cape Town. The pitstop would prove to be quite remarkable — they would have done a race-car pit team proud. The crew needed only four minutes to stop, get the parts and return to racing.

By Day 9 it was the lack of pressure that was putting pressure on all crews as they tried to harness the whispers of wind they were now experiencing. It was a weather pattern that just shouldn't have been happening at that time of year.

Ross:

Day 9 — Racing in light air would have to be the most stressful part of ocean racing. Give me 35 knots in the Southern Ocean, dodging icebergs, blasting downhill, any time. The stress: getting an extra tenth-of-a-knot of speed from the boat; making sure the crew whisper when talking; walk around the boat quietly; getting a man up the rig to search for that little vein of air; getting the right sail on; monitoring the radar every minute to plot the progress of the other boats; making sure we don't make too much fresh water at one time so the boat doesn't get heavy; making sure that we're sailing the exact wind angles. The list goes on and on. The crew are dying for the moment when the breeze strengthens and you hear the water starting to move against the hull.

Other teams were also wound up like clocks, each trying desperately to find that fraction of a knot increase in boat speed, which at the end of a four-hour watch might convert into a gain of a mile or more. Every fraction mattered, and it wasn't just the helmsman and the sail trimmers making the contributions.

Mark Rudiger — navigator, *ASSA ABLOY*:

Wind variable; mostly NNE 5–10 knots. Hold your breath. Concentrate, step gently, click, click, click, trim very slowly, barely a whisper ... the cat and mouse game is very slow but high-strung at the moment. It is night but there's a full moon. Sea's calm, light shifty winds, spinnakers setting lightly. After a week of noisy, wet sailing, five of us are now fighting for boat lengths mostly within sight of each other. Roy [Roy Heiner, skipper] is steering, anticipating every little puff while distance and bearing to the other boats is quietly relayed to him. His mind is crunching thousands of computations per minute trying to figure a way to cover all the angles for the three just behind us, and gain on Tyco just ahead. Magnus [Magnus Olsson, helmsman] watches them like a wise hawk through the binoculars while I read out the distances on the radar. At the same time, I'm downloading the latest weather models and updated surface pressure/wind tendencies. Then I run numerous scenarios on the computers to figure short-term and long-term goals. Mikey [Mike Joubert, bowman] is perched like a cat on the boom scanning the horizon for signs of wind lines. Sidney [Sidney Gavignet, helmsman] is leeward trimming the kite (spinnaker) like a fisherman trying to catch that elusive trout. Guillermo [Guillermo Altadill, sail trimmer] is watching the trim and looking for clouds that can be our friend, or our worst enemy.

When sailing in the tropics and, in particular, the equatorial regions, a single cloud can make you a hero or destroy your day. When a big cloud is forming, it is sucking in air from the windward side. On the leeward side there is no wind because it has been sucked up into the cloud; it's disappeared. So, on the windward side, you have breeze being sucked across the water surface and into the cloud, while on the leeward side there's none.

Wind conditions directly under the cloud are anyone's guess, so crews will alter course quite dramatically just to be on the windward side of a cloud. Obviously, there will be times when they can't get to the windward side so they just have to cop it. That's when they hope the cloud will literally burst and begin raining hard. In those conditions you can sail under the middle of the cloud knowing you'll get wind.

One day the crew had been pacing alongside *ASSA ABLOY* for hours, when a cloud formed ahead of them. *ASSA ABLOY* got to the windward side of it while the *News Corp* crew couldn't. Suddenly *ASSA ABLOY* was gone. They gained 10 miles on *Team News Corp* in six hours just by being on the windward side of a single cloud. 'It's a give-and-take situation,' says Ross. 'You just have to hope it goes your way the next time around.'

By Day 11 frustration was setting in. Approaching the equator, *Team News Corp* was vying for the lead with four others — *illbruck*, *Tyco*, *Amer Sports One* and *ASSA ABLOY*. *SEB* had stopped at the Canary Islands to make the repairs to its rig and *djuice dragons* had been slowed by the problems with the fitting that attaches the top of the mainsail to the mast. The female crew on *Amer Sports Too* were sailing their hardest, but had lost touch with the leaders. The unexpected light conditions continued.

Gurra Krantz — skipper, *SEB*:

What can I say? Everybody is asking what the hell we are doing out here. To be totally honest, so are we at times. We have been chasing our own tail for days now. It seems like the real weather is a little bit earlier than forecasts say.

Ian Moore — navigator, *illbruck*:

It's quite frustrating trying to sail in so little pressure. It's a bit like driving your Porsche down the motorway stuck in second gear. We have a boat that can easily top 20 knots and here we are, pootling along at six.

There was a different problem aboard *Amer Sports One* ...

Grant Dalton — skipper:

> ... *an unnamed Australian managed to throw most of the spoons over the side when he was doing the dishes. You may think this is not a problem: just use the forks. The problem is that there are no forks, just spoons, or three left, anyway. So we now need to find an imaginative way of eating, otherwise the meals are going to take an awfully long time to complete.*

The culprit was obviously the only Australian onboard, Chris Nicholson, an Olympian and world champion sailor making his debut in offshore racing. Frustration due to a lack of spoons proved to be the mother of invention. Some of the crew created extra spoons by removing the concave plastic lenses of their sunglasses and gluing them to sticks. *Voila* — a spoon! Coping with the glare was far easier than going without a spoon, an essential item for eating most freeze-dried food.

The race towards the equator and, eventually, Cape Town continued to be excruciatingly slow. Less than 1300 miles were ticked off over one six-day period, half what should have been achieved. The competitors' mental, not physical, stamina was being tested — it took 110 per cent concentration to keep moving effectively in such light winds.

Sailing in the intense heat of the tropics presented other unpleasant experiences. There was the problem of the acrid stench accumulating below deck as a result of 12 humans trying to cohabit in steamy and claustrophobic confines. Fellow watch members' sweat dripped on sleeping crew, toilets became blocked and of course there were the sweaty socks, underpants and shirts, not to mention the bodies packed below. A change of clothing was celebration time aboard *illbruck*.

Richard Clarke — helmsman/sail trimmer, *illbruck*:

> *Big day on the mighty* illbruck *as, after turning the first corner of this leg, most of us peeled to a fresh shirt. A few of us went even further and donned new boxers [underwear shorts]. With only three shirts and three pairs*

of boxers, one has to choose these moments carefully to make sure your last shirt has some life left in it at the end. This was my last shirt so I am hoping for a quick last portion of this race. Otherwise the South African authorities might quarantine me due to toxic fumes!

Around Day 13, the crew had to start thinking about food rationing as it was becoming obvious that this leg would take up to a week longer than predicted.

Grant Dalton, skipper of *Amer Sports One*, reported that they had covered just 600 miles in six days. He could not remember such a sustained period of slow going in his six previous circumnavigations.

The smooth and slow progress did, however, give crewmembers time to write more about their onboard experiences. *Team News Corp*'s sailmaker, Alby Pratt, took time to explain his multi-talented role.

Alby:

I'm one of the onboard medics — along with our bowman, Justin Slattery. Having two medics onboard each boat in the Volvo Ocean Race is compulsory. We have undergone intensive first aid training, and each boat is equipped with an extensive medical kit. With the kit and the training, we're set to treat just about every onboard ailment possible — from a nasty case of 'gunwale bum' (spotty bottom) to putting a compound fracture in traction, or performing a tracheotomy. And if there are any questions, we can video-conference a shore-based doctor who can guide us through step-by-step procedures via a camera, microphone, a satellite and the internet.

Different legs will present different problems for the medic teams. Leg One is hot and humid, which brings a range of heat-related skin problems that can be compounded by constant exposure to salt water. On Leg

Two the problems will be different. From Cape Town to Sydney we go through the notorious Southern Ocean with its sub-zero temperatures, strong winds and big seas, which increase the risk of someone doing serious damage to themselves through exposure to the cold, or breaking bones.

We've only been sailing for 13 days and already our medical kit has been pulled out, particularly for Shreda's burnt bum. The biggest problem that all medics face, though, is dealing with all the hypochondriacs onboard. For some strange reason, as soon as you volunteer for medic duty, the rest of the crew seem to think that you have just graduated from medical school and that you know all there is to know about every little pimple that may pop up on their chin!

Nick White — meteorologist, *Team News Corp*

Day 15 — Life in the navigation station has its ups and downs. On the good side, it's generally drier than on deck, but as we approach the tropics it's becoming much more pleasant on deck. No number of fans will cool it down enough down here!

For the last couple of days, I have been working on angles to the ITCZ (Inter Tropical Convergence Zone) — where to cross it and which angles to take towards Brazil. Needless to say, it's not straightforward and a bit of luck is always involved; but so far the guys seem to like what I've been suggesting. I think we're about to peel [change spinnakers], so I'd better rush on deck and find something to do.

Jez:

Day 17 — The Doldrums. So far we haven't had the drift off [racing in virtually no wind] that we had been expecting, but we certainly have had a variety of cloud-filled incidents. Last night was especially interesting, with the breeze suddenly rising to 26 knots from 8 knots. The boat changed from being comfortable to just controllable. It was good for us though; this morning we could see illbruck, ASSA and Tyco. We were in a very tight second place with ASSA.

Justin spilt some claret [blood] on the deck, but luckily there is some rain to wash it off. Can't see the other boats now so they could be engulfed in windy or windless clouds. It's very hard to tell so we will have to wait for the next sked [position report]. Seems like we are all going for the same spot to exit The Doldrums to reach the trade winds on the other side to take us down to the first island [Fernando de Noronha] that we need to round.

With all the rain in the last 48 hours it has been cooler than usual. At first the rain is a refreshing change, then it becomes tedious, especially when it's driving into your face at 26 knots, making visibility marginal. At least the fresh water makes it seem like a shower!

We're back on full rations, which has pleased the crew. Everyone is in good shape. Gone are the colds of land-based life, only to be replaced by a few skin blemishes. Our wives and girlfriends should be pleased to see us, as our controlled diet has made us look Adonis-like, with beards, though — much more effective than Jenny Craig or Weight Watchers. Have to get some clothes to fit in Cape Town, plus a steak or two, and some cheese, and some fresh bread, and some apple pie and custard and some roast lamb, and some smoked salmon...

We're halfway through this first leg and we have some hell of a yacht race, with the first four boats in sight after 14 days. As this carries on, what little hair I have left will be grey by the end.

Gundy:

Now that we are 18 days into the first leg and over half the way to Cape Town we are settled into a pretty steady routine. For the last week or so we have been sailing in very steady trade winds, which make for an even more regular schedule onboard from day to day.

Our 12 crewmembers are split into two watches of five, plus the navigators, Nick [White] and Ross [Field]. The two watches alternate sailing for four hours, then sleeping for four hours.

The food works quite easily. The on-deck watch prepares a meal at the end of each of the four hours we sail. We eat breakfast at 8am, lunch at 4pm and dinner at midnight. Justin, Joe and I take turns in preparing the meals in the last hour of our watch — depending on who is busy at the time. Alby often gets up early from his sleep and makes the lunch. The new watch then eats before they come on deck and we eat when we go down.

Tomorrow we are due at the first island we must round, so it's going to be a biggie. We're working really hard to keep the yacht in 'fast' mode. Plenty of coffee is going to be needed, I reckon. Thank God we brought plenty of that!

With the exception of Gundy and Joe Spooner, the crew had something very special to look forward to that same day — the crossing of the equator. Gundy and Joe were to be the entertainment — equator virgins. King Neptune and Queen Codfish would be visiting the yacht to induct them into the 'Crossing of the Equator' club. The fun started about 400 miles before they reached the equator.

Ross:

…The crew started terrorising the equator virgins about what was going to happen to them at the big moment. We

had specialists onboard to do that, Scotty [Jeff Scott] and Barney [Ian Walker] in particular. Scotty was right into it — he managed to put the fear of Christ into everyone. Some things happened that I just can't reveal; they have to stay with the crew. But I can say that for days before we got to the equator the guys started brewing this big broth of the most revolting stuff you can imagine, including rotten flying fish that had landed on the deck and died before we could get to them. Scotty was such a specialist that he even went to the extreme of illuminating the boat at night with the deck light so that even more flying fish would crash-land on the deck. Barney dressed up as Queen Codfish and Scotty was King Neptune. They were told that Gundy and Joe had committed heinous crimes, such as lying to the rest of the crew. They were punished accordingly — tied down, made to drink this horrible broth, then take a bite out of a dead flying fish. They were suitably welcomed into the realm of King Neptune.

As if King Neptune was welcoming the Volvo Ocean Race yachts to the southern hemisphere, the southeasterly trade winds came in at full force, but not for long, unfortunately. The pressure was starting to build. *Team News Corp* was in third place.

Ross:

We're underwater. We are reaching and pounding down through the Atlantic in a 25-knot southeasterly wind with boat speeds up to 18 knots. To make matters better, some would say worse, we're launching out of head seas left over from a depression down south. The poor yacht pounds down and when you're standing inside it feels exactly like being in an aeroplane when you hit an air pocket. Moving around the boat is hard. Your only

*options are to lie in your bunk and hold on or be on deck,
sailing. It's fantastic to be peeling off the miles like this.
I can't write much more — it's too hard to brace yourself
in the nav. station.*

Jez:

*No Sunday-morning church service today but a few wind
prayers are being said. We are just over 200 miles from
the second island we must round and we're lying just to
the west of the fleet, having made good gains by taking a
more southerly route. Ahead of us lies a large high-
pressure system and the timing of how we negotiate it
could well decide the outcome of this leg. There are
various options and a lot will happen in the next 24 to 48
hrs ... so don't go away. As always, heaps of effort is being
put into working out a solution and working the boat to
give us the best chance to get it right. Spirits are high with
tense anticipation.*

When you are out of sight of your opponents in this race it's like you're
trying to punch an opponent in the dark. You must keep trying your hardest
and hope that you connect. The end of each round is every six hours when
the position reports come in from the other yachts.

Ross:

*The six-hourly skeds are as stressful as being investigated
by the tax department every six hours: Have you done
that right? How did you make a gain there? How did you
make a loss there? Have you declared everything that you
have gained? Shall we suffer a loss here to make a gain
there? And it goes on. We are coming into the island of
Trindade (300 miles east of Rio de Janeiro), which we
have to round to port. We have suffered a loss coming into
the island: our westerly and southerly option dried up.*

The gains weren't there any longer and we had to regroup, take a loss and join the fleet again. It's painful and frustrating because all those miles we have lost were hard-fought, but there's no use in crying over it, because we still have plenty of miles left to drag back illbruck *and* ASSA ABLOY *and to pull away from* Tyco.

A distinct lack of wind was only one of the problems faced aboard *Team News Corp*. There was bartering to deal with. Ah, the things that really mattered ...

Gundy:

Day 24 — Let's put the yacht race aside for just one moment and get down to the real issues. After 22 days at sea and 11 remaining with only freeze-dried food and one set of clothes, what is a valuable commodity? Coffee? Nicotine? Chocolate?

Coffee we have plenty of — one packet a day between here and Cape Town, not to mention the odd packet of Milo and enough tea to sink a US Navy battle group. So we're OK there.

Nicotine: Now here's where it starts to get interesting. We have two smokers onboard and their supplies are beginning to fade away. Scotty, who stashed a packet or so in each day's food bag, has got to Day 31 already, while Barney has a few packets and one cigar left. Both have taken to scouring the boat for lost packets and interrogating suspected thieves — of which there are several.

Things have taken a more interesting turn after Scotty rummaged through the remaining food bags. He has discovered that on Day 25 we have Kit-Kat bars — one giant bar each. This is our first chocolate since the start and the discovery has led to a blossoming black market onboard. Scotty has offered his Kit-Kat to the highest

Top *Team News Corp* glides across the Hudson River with New York City as the backdrop. During the four-week stay in New York the yacht was christened and the News Corp international staff incentive program based around the campaign was announced. *Richard Langdon/Ocean Images*

Bottom Dwarfed by New York's World Trade Centre towers just a month before the September 11 terrorist attacks, skipper Jez Fanstone helms *Team News Corp* during a corporate promotion day. *Richard Langdon/Ocean Images*

Left As a tribute to America following September 11, the Stars and Stripes flies from the forestay of *Team News Corp* on the morning of the Volvo Ocean Race (VOR) start in Southampton.

Top About to take on the world. The 12 members of the *Team News Corp* crew line up on deck on the morning of the race start.

Bottom left I love my Dad. Ian 'Barney' Walker and his three-year-old daughter, Michaela, enjoy the farewell in Southampton.

Bottom right Jez gives some tips on steering to the yacht's unofficial 13th crewmember, Bart Simpson.

All images *Richard Langdon/Ocean Images*

Top The world is round. *Team News Corp*, in the foreground, heads away from Southampton on Leg One to Cape Town. *Richard Langdon/Ocean Images*

Bottom left A wet welcome to racing around the world for the crew of *djuice dragons* as they battle head winds off the coast of Portugal. *djuice dragons*

Bottom right Jeff 'Scotty' Scott displays his tools of trade as he prepares to become a galley slave a few days out from Southampton. *Team News Corp*

Top left Dolphins escort *djuice* towards Cape Town. *djuice dragons*

Top right King Neptune and Queen Codfish's handiwork during an induction for three *Team SEB* crewmembers crossing the equator for the first time. *Team SEB*

Centre left *Team News Corp* is partially submerged by a wave while being pressed hard under spinnaker. *Richard Langdon/Ocean Images*

Centre right Joe Spooner's head injury receives attention after *Team News Corp* arrives in Cape Town. *Richard Langdon/Ocean Images*

Bottom left After a month at sea eating freeze-dried food, Steve Cotton's first meal in Cape Town was a birthday cake. *Richard Langdon/Ocean Images*

Bottom right Bart Simpson supervises 'Wazza' working on *Team News Corp* in Cape Town. *Richard Langdon/Ocean Images*

Top En route to Sydney. With Cape Town's Table Mountain dominating the scene, the VOR fleet heads south for the first taste of the Southern Ocean. *Richard Langdon/Ocean Images*

Bottom left A close call for *Team News Corp* during a tacking duel off Cape Town. *Richard Langdon/Ocean Images*

Bottom right Just an average act for Justin Slattery as he is hoisted aloft on a misty day to replace a broken mainsail batten on *Team News Corp*. *Team News Corp*

Right top Fogbound. *Tyco, Team News Corp, illbruck, djuice* and *Amer Sports One* slice their way through a shallow layer of fog one hour out of Cape Town after the start of Leg Two. *Daniel Forster, illbruck*

Right bottom The *Team News Corp* crew start to get that cold and wet feeling as they approach the Cape of Good Hope during Leg Two. *Richard Langdon/Ocean Images*

Top Inhospitable territory for *Amer Sports One* as the fleet heads for Sydney. *Rick Tomlinson*
Bottom *Tyco* is hammered while heading into the Roaring Forties south of Cape Town. *Rick Tomlinson*

bidder. Alby kicked off with an offer of two cigarettes, and after some hushed whispering, Justin has topped him with three. So far, only one packet of the valuable cigarettes has reared its head, however ... I happen to know the location of a large quantity of the Scandinavian treat SNUSS (chewing tobacco). One tin can last a couple of days and this particular stash consists of several tins!

There is a good chance I am going to be eating well between here and Cape Town ... yes, snacks for three people once I've traded the SNUSS! Which also puts me in a pretty strong position with all the big eaters onboard; for instance, a snack is probably worth two beers from Joe Spooner when we get to Cape Town. All I have to do now is hold out until the 25th so that I can be sure everyone else has played their hand — then it's just a question of 'How much is a nicotine fix worth to you, buddy?'

Bring on Cape Town, where I can reap the rewards of my cunning foresight — hamburgers, beer and sushi.

After being at sea for more than three weeks it appears that even hardened ocean-racing sailors become little more than big kids when it comes to treats. Trying to keep everyone happy while dealing out the goodies brings a new dimension to the racing.

Ross:

As you can imagine, stress levels are rather high at a time like this. Wind from all directions, losing miles, then gaining miles and trying to work out the best part of the ocean to be in. These major decisions need to be made by the navigator, skipper and watch captains.

On a slightly lighter note, the crew, right at this moment, have two major decisions to make:

1. Counting out the lollies [sweets] to ensure that everyone gets exactly the same ... but 12 crew into 50 lollies doesn't go; so what is done with the remaining two lollies? Do we throw them over the side to avoid a major dispute?

2. Which kitchen brush is used for the dishes and which is used as a toilet brush? They are both the same colour and ended up close to the galley, and the galley is very close to the toilet...

The leg turned upside down soon after Trindade was rounded. *Amer Sports One* had the benefit of seeing the four leading yachts lying ahead, looking like wind vanes showing just what was happening with the breeze. They were 'parked' in near windless holes all over the ocean. Skipper Grant Dalton did everything that anyone in his position would do: he analysed the situation ahead, found the passing lane and slotted his red-and-grey-hulled racer into a big lead in a very short time. *ASSA ABLOY*, which led handsomely at the island and looked set to show the way to Cape Town, went to the east and found a vacuum instead of wind. They fell from first to fifth place. John Kostecki's *illbruck* wriggled its way out of the calm and moved slowly south in second spot, with *Team News Corp* third. It was hellish racing for all crews. Only *Team SEB* and *djuice dragons*, both slowed by equipment failure, were out of the hunt, along with Lisa McDonald's team on *Amer Sports Too*.

The fact that *Amer Sports One* was leading came as a surprise to Grant Dalton. '[Navigator] Roger Nilson and I have been burnt many times by boats getting south of us, picking up breeze and disappearing,' he says. 'In fact, it happened to us in exactly the same place four years ago. So we came round Trindade, headed south, no questions, no discussion — not making that mistake again ... and suddenly we ended up in the lead, albeit a very fragile one.

'So we accepted the gift with due humbleness. The next 24 hours would be most interesting, but we liked the south ...'

Ross:

Day 26 — Fingers crossed. Right now, we're sliding along nicely, doing 14–16 knots in a 16-knot northeasterly making great miles to Cape Town, which is about 2000 miles away. Amer Sports One is dead ahead with illbruck just behind her. Since the disaster at the island [Trindade], in which Amer Sports One did the 'billy goat' around the outside of those of us who were parked (it pays to be behind sometimes), it has been a case of the rich getting richer, with the front boats sailing into more pressure [stronger winds]. Fortunately, we're one of those front boats!

We're starved onboard for information from the outside world. We discuss the limited news that comes in at length. Of course, the crisis in Afghanistan is high on the agenda and, being an Australian entry in the Volvo Ocean Race, we were all very pleased to hear that Australia is supporting the US and England. We might be hungry, dirty, frustrated and uncomfortable out here, but it's very safe.

Jez and his team were desperate to consolidate on their third placing. The breeze they had scoured the horizon to find finally arrived and began to propel them towards their target — Cape Town. The challenge was to get away from the hunters coming up from behind and to hunt down the two ahead.

Ross:

We're on our way, doing 16.5 knots with a shy kite [spinnaker] in a 22-knot wind. I can hear the water powering over the deck, Scottie steering, Joe and Jez on the pumps [coffee grinder winches], Gundy trimming (and talking) and Justin on the mainsail.

The rest of the crew are down below sleeping and Alby is getting lunch ready. Nick's asleep so I'm in the navigation station looking at computer screens, working out where we should or shouldn't be going.

Everything is normal. We're praying that we are finally putting miles on the other two boats ahead. I hope like hell the rich stop getting richer. It's frustrating because I know that we have the fastest boat ...

Food and our cooking gas are getting short but I am sure we'll get to Cape Town without starving. We can't have hot coffee or tea any more, as the gas has to be conserved for cooking. Cold coffee is the call of the day and we pretend that it's hot — just to annoy Gundy, the gas/food policeman.

The gas/food policeman had his own thoughts on his dilemmas in the catering department ...

Gundy:

Over the many years I've anticipated doing this race I often wondered what I would crave the most nearing the end of a really long leg like this one. I can now tell you the answer — I JUST WANT TO GET THERE!

Burgers would be great on the dock or, even better, we'll finish early in the morning and have a huge breakfast with heaps of sausages and baked beans, a damn good wash in steaming hot water, sleep in a nice bed for 10 hours and we'll wear nice, clean, dry clothes — all these things would be great. But without a doubt, the thing I most crave is the sight of Table Mountain and the realisation that the leg is over.

It seems more and more likely that the guys out in front are gone — they've got us beaten. We just hope that we are 'gone' from the boats behind!

A short while before we started in the UK (which is a month ago tomorrow), I got handed the food program. So far, everything is going alright, but we are definitely going to run out at some stage before the finish. The extent of the shortage will just depend on how long it takes to get there. One thing is for sure: I will never do the food on a race like this again after this one is over! Imagine telling 11 guys that they have no lunch today. Everyone onboard has a different idea about how the rationing should be done and I am copping an earful from every direction. The only course seems to be to let it run and see how we go.

Arriving on the dock in a week's time will be fantastic (assuming we do get there), and no matter how bad our predicament seems, we only have to look at the latest sked, see how far behind the last group of boats is, and take comfort in the fact that we will be resting up while they are still racing.

It wasn't just Gundy who was impatient about reaching Cape Town. A month at sea was taking its toll and the entire crew was getting restless, making Ross's job even more difficult.

Ross:

Any parent who has taken their children on a long trip will appreciate what every navigator is going through right now — endless questions: 'When will we be there?', 'What time will we arrive?', 'Where are we staying?', 'I'm hungry . . .'

We have 1323 miles to a buoy in Table Bay, and then 0.85 mile from there to the finish. Amer Sports One and illbruck have got away from us, missing the light spot we found, but we are now extending on Tyco and ASSA ABLOY. We were just a little too far behind when the front came through. This, combined with a broken sail, has meant that we haven't been able to hold on. But we haven't given up. The fat lady hasn't sung yet, but she's moving out onto the stage. We have some moves up our sleeves, so stand by.

Onboard the daily routine is as usual: sailing, sleeping and Jeff Scott complaining that someone is stealing his thermals (they are usually lying in the bilge). Steve Cotton refuses to continue sharing a crew bag with him for the Southern Ocean leg (and I agree with him). Gundy has put his toys back in the pram after yesterday's spit about the food/gas, but Joe continues to try to wind him up ... and he's good at it. Joe leaves us in Cape Town to continue sailing with the Team New Zealand *America's Cup campaign. Of course, he's getting stick from the guys about being a wimp — that he's scared of the Southern Ocean.*

Alby has solved the world's problems on this leg and is looking for a job with the UN after the race.

After one month at sea on a painfully slow leg with 12 humans trying to cohabit in a self-imposed prison cell-like situation, the stress factor was rising on all boats. Energy was fading, especially on *djuice dragons*, which was at the back of the pack — they hadn't recovered from a slow start and equipment failure. Assistant navigator Wouter Verbraak told how when the crew became tired and frustrated it was easy to forget about asking questions nicely, keeping a smile on your face and being considerate and tolerant towards fellow crewmembers. 'To me, this is one of the most fascinating things in our sport. The winning crew is the one that does not lose sight of the important things, especially when things aren't going well. Winning is easy. What matters is what you do when things are not going well.'

As they neared Cape Town the *Team News Corp* crew were running out of options when it came to catching the leaders. But, barring equipment failure or totally unforeseen circumstances, third place was looking very safe; a highly commendable result considering they had been ranked as outsiders at the start.

The advantage *Amer Sports One* had gained days earlier was being ground down by *illbruck*. An enthralling battle was unfolding — in which a master of the oceans was defending against a challenge from a relative newcomer to endurance racing. Kiwi Grant Dalton, *Amer Sports One*'s skipper, a veteran of five Whitbread round-the-world races and winner of The Race — a 62-day nonstop sprint around the globe on a giant catamaran — was seeing his lead eroded by American John Kostecki, an Olympic medallist and America's Cup sailor who was adapting to this passage like the proverbial duck to water. Dalton had chosen a crew that combined round-the-world racing experience with the power and enthusiasm of youth, but sometimes there were problems with the blend. Approaching Cape Town the master didn't hold back in delivering a very public verbal spray.

Grant Dalton:

> *The last 24 hours has been a reality check for this team on what is going to happen to us in the Southern Ocean, unless we go back to basics on how to sail a boat like this in a lot of breeze under spinnaker. It has left us with two totally destroyed spinnakers, one of which is mainly 150 miles behind us, a broken internal halyard and a crew who are now somewhat more receptive to the wise old men onboard telling them what to do.*
>
> *Last night in a squall we broached in a spectacular wipeout in 27 knots of breeze with our full-size heavy runner [spinnaker] and a full-size staysail [set]. We lay there, horizontal, for 20 seconds until the staysail halyard broke, firing the staysail through the spinnaker. When the boat righted we pulled the undamaged staysail onboard and the 20 per cent of the remaining spinnaker. In the pitch-black we reset our (other) heavy runner, which is small, and waited for the mileage damage at the coming sked. As expected, a slick, well-prepared illbruck, sailing much better, wiped 7 miles off our lead.*
>
> *The night before that, in an aborted watch change during which the new helmsman was not orientated and the team were just standing round, we wiped out and*

blew out our reaching [across the wind] Code 3 spinnaker. We're going to miss this sail in the next few days — we're heading into moderate reaching conditions. The sailmakers are desperately trying to fix it but the damage is very bad and it won't end up being particularly strong.

... The tropics can spoil you and now, as we enter the fringes of the Southern Ocean, the problems we've had will serve as a notice of what lies ahead ...

I am amazed at how fortunate we have been with the weather, and how unlucky most of the others have been. I know how it feels (from past experiences). It just surrounds you and unless you are strong, will rip your very soul apart. You cannot escape the sked, you cannot escape the fact that when you steer, when you change a sail, when you try to sleep, this feeling of utter helplessness is swamping you. Maybe other people don't think that way, but I doubt it, as we are all competitive sportsmen out here and competing hard drives us.

Then you have to come ashore, face the questions, put on a brave face, then get up off the canvas for the next leg. Now here's the greatest part: you come back stronger than before. When wounded, an animal is at its most powerful and dangerous. The campaigns with the worst results in this leg are the ones that are to be feared the most en route to Sydney.

The weather conditions at Trindade meant that the eight racing yachts were scattered all over the South Atlantic. In pure sailing time, there was more than a week between first and last. *illbruck* did manage to pass *Amer Sports One* in the closing stages, while *Team News Corp* maintained third position. But before the boats arrived in the city they call the Tavern of the Seas, the weather became malevolent once more. A savage southeasterly wind gusting to 50 knots whipped up vicious waves that peaked at 35 feet.

Team News Corp's Barney Walker, one of the most experienced heavy weather sailors onboard, said it was some of the worst upwind sailing he'd ever encountered. The yacht literally launched itself off one wave in a way that Ross Field had never experienced in all his years at sea: 'We went up this huge wave and just kept going up. There was nothing behind it except air — the back was as vertical as the face ... it was like driving a car over a cliff. I've no doubt that the only thing still in the water was the tip of the rudder. I'm sure even the keel and bulb [depth 13 feet] were completely out of the water and in midair. The crash was unbelievable when we landed. It was like landing 30 000 pounds on concrete. I couldn't believe that nothing broke.'

One more drama tested the team before they arrived in Cape Town.

Alby:

> A big wave washed across the deck and took Joe Spooner with it. He smashed his head on a deck fitting and came to a rapid halt. This knocked him out for a few seconds, then he came down below with blood pouring everywhere. We put him in a bunk and had a look at the wound — a really nasty cut just above his ear. 'Ah, this is going to need stitches,' I thought. 'Time for Dr Alby and Dr Justin to go to work.' It was really difficult because the boat was bashing around all over the ocean in a 50-knot wind. If a wound needed only a couple of stitches we had been told it was best not to use anaesthetic; so I held his head still while Justin did the deed with the needle. Joe wasn't really happy about that, but we assured him it would hurt more to get the anaesthetic. It was a two-man operation — Justin put the needle through one side and I pulled it out the other, then tied the knot. The two stitches went in really well, actually, but because the boat was jumping around so much they weren't the straightest.

All yachts were taking a savage hammering and while the leaders closed in on Cape Town, those towards the tail could look forward to another week of bashing and crashing to windward. Emma Westmacott, a watch leader on the all-female crew aboard *Amer Sports Too*, did manage to get to the computer to tell the world about a day at the office.

Emma:

> Tap, tap, tap. 'Em,' I hear, and I peer out of the sleeping bag to a sorry but smiling face (it's time to go on watch). I lie in bed and can hear spray cascading across the decks, the bow launching up off a wave and thundering back down, bellyflopping into the sea beneath. I hear the faint sound of voices, 'Bad wave on the bow,' the groan of the sheet being eased on the winch, the bubbling and swishing of water rattling past the hull, and the jolting of the entire boat as it pounds along. Shutting the eyes again is not an option; sleep would just engulf me despite the commotion. I look over the edge of the bunk. It's a long way down to the floor: how best do I roll over the edge and not end up on the floor way down to leeward? Oh my goodness, where are all my clothes? Locating personal stuff is a nightmare if gear is moved around to trim [balance] the boat better; it's always best to sleep with everything. Grab a boot and shove it on, then the other. The floor is wet; I hate wet socks. Clamber up the front; find the rail with the 'foulies' [wet weather clothing] hanging on it. Count 1, 2, 3, 4, 5 hooks. There is my gear. It's hard to get the jacket and pants off the hook while being bounced around. On goes the kettle and the generator is rattling away. Must go to the loo before getting togged up. It's impossible afterwards.
>
> Next I sit on the floor in the dark (we've run out of torch batteries, and the cabin lights distract the driver) and battle to put on my on-deck clothing, including wet weather gear. Everything is a bit sore from permanently being salty — eyes, hands. I crawl back to the nav. station to see what's

new: Where are we? Where are the others? What is our aim this watch? Then up on deck ... Beating to windward is what we're doing, on the wind, pounding along, keeping the boat rolling, keeping the speed up, keeping up the height [closest course possible to the direction of the wind]. Must keep everyone focused: trimming, driving and keeping the wolves [the opposition] from the door. Bellies, I might add, getting slightly hungry, as we have started to ration food. We're trundling along to Cape Town.

To the south the pain was about to end for *Team News Corp*. With early-morning mist shrouding Cape Town's famous backdrop, Table Mountain, and nary a wisp of wind ruffling the surface of the bay, *Team News Corp* coasted towards the finish line. It was an entirely grey scene, with soft, low cloud hanging like a canopy over the city and the water. Third place was secure, but how long it would take the team to ghost across the line was anyone's guess. The calm closed in on them like a giant clam as they entered the bay, and in doing so turned an estimated two-hour run to the line into an exasperating eight-hour saga. Shore crew, family and friends, spectators and the official party waited to welcome them, and waited, and waited. When the tip of the mast and mainsail finally came into view over the top of the distant waterfront buildings, you could make out a black dot in the rig. It was Shreda. He'd been sent aloft to scout for wind and report back to the crew below. His eyes were scanning 360 degrees, searching for patches of ripples on the near-glassy surface — evidence of breeze.

The torment continued until a loud horn on the finish boat confirmed it was all over. The mental pain they had endured over the final stage was quickly forgotten when this tired-looking, bearded and noticeably thinner crew guided their blue and white charge into the dock to rousing cheers and an eardrum-bursting blast of the yacht's battle song.

Nutritionist Jan van der Lee's first impression was how thin they all looked. It was a worry. Smiley had lost a lot of weight and so had Alby, who'd had no extra padding to lose when he left England. She would have to rethink the food provisions for the next leg.

The media pack converged on the side of the yacht, wanting comments from Jez and Ross. Their bloodshot eyes were evidence of the water blasting they'd copped in the past three days.

Jez:

> We had everything from zero to 50 knots. The boys did a great job. The boat's fast — we're on the podium and that's where we wanted to be on the first leg. It's a job well done by everyone.
>
> The leg was very intense and took its toll. If we took our clothes off you'd see what the food rationing's done for us. I'm about six kilos lighter … we didn't have any food for the last 24 hours, but we were mentally prepared for that.

Ross:

> We were very unfortunate to fall off the back of the weather system that got the two other yachts here ahead of us. We wrecked a sail that was valuable to us and lost ground that we just couldn't recover. Dropping half a knot of boat speed when we lost the sail meant that they just crept away, and it was the end of any chance we had of catching them.

More importantly for Ross, though, were some issues aboard that had become apparent during the leg. As campaign director, he was concerned about Jez's approach as skipper, which was probably due to his lack of experience in this environment. He felt that Jez had given the crew a bit too much of a free rein. These concerns had gnawed at him for much of the time at sea and they had to be dealt with. Within 48 hours of arriving in Cape Town the two sat down to discuss the problem. Partners as they were, they reached a mutually satisfying agreement.

Ross:

> I'm taking over the boat and will run it while it's sailing. Jez, who agrees with this, will stay onboard and, as far as

the world is concerned, will be seen to be the skipper. The
crew knows about the change but it's not the business of
anyone else, especially the media.

Things were far worse aboard *ASSA ABLOY*, which came fifth after going out on a tangent, hitting a calm and losing what appeared to be an insurmountable lead. There were reports of high tension onboard between skipper Roy Heiner and other senior members of the crew. The syndicate backing the boat sacked Heiner and replaced him with crewmember Neal McDonald, husband of *Amer Sports Too* skipper Lisa McDonald. Navigator Mark Rudiger stayed as co-skipper.

As dramatic as Heiner's dismissal was, crew changes were to be very much part of this race. With nine widely varying legs making up the total course some skippers had structured their teams so specialist helmsmen, sail trimmers and tacticians could be brought on as required.

Far more interesting and controversial was a protest lodged by the Race Committee questioning the legality of modifications to *illbruck*. It was discovered that a weed-cutting device had been attached to the leading edge of the propeller unit and that the unit itself was streamlined with a filling compound. Rules governing the VO 60 class of yacht state: 'Only modifications to specified machinery approved by the chief measurer are permitted.' The chief measurer had not approved these modifications and, as such, it was believed that *illbruck* did not comply with the rules.

The protest was upheld but, much to the amazement of the majority of competitors and race followers, instead of receiving a time or place penalty, the *illbruck* team was fined a mere £1500.

≪ With 6550 nautical miles of rugged ocean lying ahead, *Team News Corp* leaves Cape Town bound for Sydney.
Richard Langdon/Ocean Images

CAPE TOWN TO SYDNEY

You have to go into yourself and control your own fear. I actually enjoy it, being on the edge. It's 99 per cent risk.

JEFF SCOTT — WATCH LEADER, *TEAM NEWS CORP*

the two calamities the crews feared most when racing were falling overboard or the yacht hitting something at high speed, suffering a catastrophic structural failure and sinking. These dangers were at their most intense level on the legs into the fearsome Southern Ocean.

Leg Two was a 6550-mile dive deep into the icy wilderness where, more often than not, the world's worst sailing conditions will be encountered. This is where icebergs, snowstorms and massive waves can trap the unwary. The fleet's destination via this inhospitable territory was Sydney, Australia, and by the time the leg was over there were stories of busted bones and medical emergencies, a broken rudder, a near sinking, two world distance records, spectacular wipeouts, a remarkable tactical blunder and stunningly close racing.

Cape Town had been a wonderful host city for more than two weeks, but because of September 11 the atmosphere around the Victoria and Alfred Docks was subdued. There had been an understandable reluctance by the majority of would-be guests of yacht sponsors to travel from Europe and North America to enjoy the planned corporate hospitality. As a result, sponsors significantly reduced, or entirely abandoned, their promotion agendas.

During the stop some of the *Team News Corp* crew flew to their respective homes around the world for family and business commitments, while others stayed and prepared the boat for the next start. Oli and the shore crew removed the mast for a complete overhaul and had the yacht craned out of the water so the hull and keel could be faired and repainted.

Jez and Ross were keen to keep the crew fit, so under the guidance of Leah, who is a professional trainer, most days started with light exercises and a high-spirited game of touch football in a park adjacent to the crew accommodation. Once the yacht was back in the water a sail-testing program commenced — the sails are the engine, so they must be perfect.

Because it was going to blow hard and the leg would be primarily downwind, they took off some of their largest masthead spinnakers and replaced them with smaller, fractional sails (which set from a point about 90 per cent of the way up the mast). They did a test program before departure to decide what their final sail wardrobe would be. They also did a program aimed at improving their upwind speed. They felt they had a shortcoming in the 13–16-knot wind range, so they worked on a new overlapping headsail that would wrap around the (mast) stays. Loading the boat differently, putting a bit more weight down aft, was another strategy. And they took a little more food because they were going to burn a lot more calories in the Southern Ocean. Going into the second leg they felt they had a boat that could do the job and that with modifications and revamping they could pull it off.

Jez:

Four or five boats will be very close on this next leg and I expect we'll be one of them. As a crew we certainly haven't done many miles down there in the Southern Ocean, but as individuals we have. If we can keep the pedal to the metal we'll be in good shape.

Joe Spooner returned to Auckland to resume training with the Kiwi America's Cup defence team, so the crew of *Team News Corp* was reinforced with the inclusion of the highly talented Irish offshore sailor, and now Australian resident, Gordon Maguire. 'I gathered that Ross and Jez were a little concerned about the Southern Ocean, and the youthfulness of their crew. They wanted a little bit of adult tuition, I guess, just to make sure everything went tickety boo. I certainly needed some convincing to do it,' he said. 'Having done the race three times I knew that it was dangerous, and being married now, with two young children, I made a positive decision early on not to do the race this time. I was over it. Also, in a sport like this life doesn't begin at 40. I was 40. You get hurt: you get hurt for weeks. You pull muscles that you didn't even know you had. It gets to the point where you have to be a bit careful. But, despite my theories, Leg Two made sense for me. I live in Sydney and the leg was from Cape Town to home. I could go away from home for two or three weeks for a bit part — walk on, walk off. Easy. So I signed on.'

The sheer, 1000-metre-high craggy rock face of Table Mountain was absorbing the early morning sun on 11 November when the crews gathered on the dock, ready to step aboard the yachts they would be calling home for the next 25 days. The decks and the dockside became a vivid spectrum of colour as spinnakers were carefully spread then packed in their bags in anticipation of the crazy downwind rides that would come within days. Each crewmember's personal gear bag also took on new and larger proportions; crammed with thermal clothing and other anti-freeze attire.

With every sailor well aware of the dangers they would be facing over the next three to four weeks there was a heightened air of emotion associated with the farewells this time. When wives, partners, families and friends embraced, the tears welled and flowed.

> **Gurra Krantz — skipper, *Team SEB*:**
>
> *These round-the-world races are different from any other racing. The emotional farewells you see on the dock are really touching. Saying the casual 'bye bye' to my daughter, Emma, tore my heart out. If somebody asked me that very moment if I really wanted to go, I would not be true to myself if I said 100 per cent 'Yes'. Then we hide bravely behind sentiments like 'It is part of the game' or something else equally stupid. When I am finally racing, that is what I want to do, but no doubt it is costing at the other end.*

It was a case of ladies first when the time came for the eight yachts to drop off the mooring lines and depart. Lisa McDonald and her crew aboard *Amer Sports Too* showed the way out, the arrangement being that the yachts would leave the dock at four-minute intervals in the reverse order of their arrival into Cape Town. All superfluous equipment — such as mooring lines, fenders, the national flag and flagstaff — was either left on the dock or passed over to support boats prior to the start.

A 20-knot southeasterly wind welcomed the yachts onto the waters of Table Bay. Sails were hoisted, settings checked and the angle of the start line to the wind analysed. Every second can count in this type of racing, and getting the jump on the opposition — even at this early stage of such a long leg — could make a significant difference at the end.

When the starting signal boomed out at 1pm the dogfight for the honour of being first out of the bay began. It appeared that at some stage each yacht held the upper hand, sometimes momentarily, but when the outer rounding mark was reached it was *Team News Corp* leading by 30 seconds from *illbruck* and *djuice dragons*. The contest took on an eerie atmosphere when a shallow sea mist descended on the course. Each yacht's rig cut a swathe through the thick air.

Bows were pointed south towards the Cape of Good Hope and the Southern Ocean. As the fleet disappeared into the fog some crewmembers reflected on their departure; others on what might lie ahead.

Shreda:
> From the start we were on fire sailing upwind. The fact
> that everyone had a chance of leading and Team News
> Corp *finished up in front was pretty radical.*

Within hours it was apparent that this would not be a soft start for the sailors. The situation could be likened to putting a small toy boat in a washing machine on the 'heavy wash' cycle. The horrendous conditions pitched at the fleet were particularly testing on the helmsmen, who had to combine racing skills with seamanship; in pitch darkness they had to sense the motion of every 20-foot wave, guide the yacht up and over it, then do their very best to avoid a boat-breaking crash on the other side.

Ross:
> That would have to be my worst first night at sea for a
> long time. Big seas, on the wind, bashing and crashing
> into a 38-knot southeasterly, crew seasick, no one eating,
> inside of the boat a shambles. Horrible ...
> We have been sailing our planned route — heading
> south as quickly as possible (while the others stayed to the
> east), and I believe it will pay off. We have advanced

south on the fleet and it's encouraging to see them now following our track. Time will tell — we're comfortable with our plan.

Stu Wilson — sail trimmer, *ASSA ABLOY*:

Most of us were thinking, 'What is wrong with us that makes us want to do this?!' I left my girlfriend, good food, a dry bed and a hot shower to bang around out here struggling with wet Kevlar sails and 12 smelly guys. Even though the boat has been made more comfortable with the addition of new sleeping bags and midlayers, it was hard not to dream of all the home comforts while holding yourself in your bunk, trying to sleep that first uncomfortable night.

The Roaring Forties had opened the front door ahead of schedule and greeted the fleet in the Southern Ocean in a most unwelcoming fashion. The line between racing and seamanship was becoming even finer and the possibility of damage came with every wave, as race favourite *illbruck* was to discover.

John Kostecki — skipper, *illbruck*:

We were changing to our smaller heavy air jib as the wind built up to between 30 and 35 knots. Then, all of a sudden, we noticed that the boat was not going very well and felt sluggish. The bow seemed to be lower than normal and it started taking waves more frequently. Rosco [Ross Halcrow, the sail trimmer] went below deck to check the bow hatch, to see if we had a water problem. He came back on deck with a fright — he hadn't been able to open the hatch because of the amount of water in the forward tank ahead of the watertight bulkhead. The boat got slower and slower, then we couldn't keep her going any more. We went into irons [stopped involuntarily with the sails flapping] as we were trying to figure out why the bow was sinking so fast. We eventually discovered that an inspection port on the bow, just behind the headstay, had somehow come off. The entire forward tank was full of water and we had to stop racing. We dropped the jib, moved all of the gear below and above deck as far aft as possible to stop the bow from sinking further, then started the emergency pump and bailed with buckets from on deck. It took nearly two hours to control the situation before we could begin racing again.

It was a frightening moment for us, especially as we didn't initially know why the water was coming in so fast. Did we have a hole in the hull below or near the waterline? We had thoughts of going back to shore to smoother, calmer waters, but fortunately we were able to control the situation out at sea. We were very lucky to come out of last night losing only 20 miles. Hopefully we can stay in touch and get back into the race.

Kostecki was to confirm when he arrived in Sydney that, at one stage, the crew were almost convinced the yacht was going to sink.

Team News Corp continued its bold charge south, splitting from the pack and remaining on a very determined course. The yacht wasn't receiving the conveyor belt ride from the current that the others were enjoying, but it was being lined up for a better angle of attack on the blocking high-pressure ridge that lay ahead. If the *News Corp* strategists were right and the conditions didn't change, they could break through the ridge first and sail into the Roaring Forties ahead of the rest. The spinnaker would go up and they would be as good as gone.

The rest of the fleet were enjoying a close race with *Team Tyco* leading — until skipper Kevin Shoebridge made a highly emotional satellite phone call to race headquarters. The Volvo Ocean Race had its first major casualty. *Team Tyco* was turning back.

Kevin Shoebridge:

Earlier today we were sailing along in about 25 knots of breeze, when we heard a loud bang at the back of the boat. It was quickly clear that the problem was with the rudder — when we inspected it we realised that some of the carbon taping on the front of the rudder shaft had let go. About an hour ago we heard another bang, much louder this time. The rudder shaft is very close to sheering off. It has become very unstable with no sideways support and it looks as if it will basically just snap. We have pulled the sails down and the emergency rudder is going over the back. We have all the emergency equipment ready, along with the pumping equipment, and we've sealed all the watertight doors. Now we'll just wait for daylight and make a plan. We'll probably have to head back to South Africa.

Shoebridge was obviously near tears when he made the call. There was no way the yacht could sail safely for nearly 5000 miles to the Western Australian coast. The safety of the crew had to be considered. There was only one option: to sail very cautiously back to Port Elizabeth, 750 miles upwind, and arrange to ship *Team Tyco* to Sydney, where repairs would be made.

The weather didn't play into *Team News Corp*'s court as much as they'd hoped but the consolation was that while they hadn't gained, they hadn't lost. They were still very much in the running and there was a chance that their southerly course could still bring dividends in the days ahead.

Ross:

Day 6 — At the moment the six-hourly skeds are crucial for confirming our weather data. There is more pressure in the south as we predicted and we are making nice gains on the fleet. It's very encouraging and we believe we'll continue to make small gains until things even out later. We have good separation, which enables us to go faster when we like without giving away the south advantage we have earned.

We are running under spinnaker and waiting for a front to come through to give us strong west/northwest winds later tomorrow. The crew are enjoying sailing without the constant spray flying over the deck, but occasionally the bow dives under, sending a river of water charging down the deck. Everything on the boat is packed down at the back and the crew are sleeping in the aft bunks — all in a bid to help keep the bow from nosediving. We're travelling at speeds up to 22 knots but averaging around 17 knots. Really nice sailing.

As they sailed deeper into the Southern Ocean the fleet entered iceberg territory. For first-timers, the sighting of the first 'berg was an unforgettable experience.

Shreda:

I was off watch below deck when I heard the call 'Iceberg!' go out. I leapt out of my bunk and rushed up on deck to see this iceberg pass about a mile to our port side. Awesome. When I got back to my bunk then there was a second call. I dashed back onto the deck and, sure enough, half a mile to starboard was another one. I was getting a little apprehensive, wondering what we were doing to avoid these icebergs and what would happen when the sun went down. By the time we spotted the third iceberg, which was during my next watch, I wasn't feeling too comfortable at all. I poked my head down below and said to Nick White at the nav. station, 'Can you see this thing on the radar?' 'See what?' he asked. After that, I couldn't sleep during my off watch. I managed to lie in my pipe cot, gripping onto the bars on the side, tense and a little concerned for my safety. I was also seen running forward and checking the watertight bulkheads, just in case we found an iceberg suddenly in the middle of the night.

Jez:

Day 6 — It's another grey day in the Southern Ocean, but onboard the atmosphere is bright as we reel in the leaders who are now only 30 miles ahead. We are still well to the south and in better wind so we should take more miles in the next sked.

The conditions are good for downwind sailing at the moment with full-size sails, averaging over 17 knots. Our quality of life has been vastly improved by the effectiveness of the survival suits in these conditions, and there is the outside chance of getting towards being dry!

We had spaghetti bolognaise for lunch, which is always a winner. Saw our third iceberg and passed within 670 feet of a growler that was downwind of it. Seen enough of those now, thank you.

The further the fleet sailed south, the colder and more miserable the environment became. The air and sea temperature hovered just above freezing. The blinding spray hit like showers of bullets. There was sleet and sometimes snow. Survival suits provided the best protection in these environs, but the cold still made even small tasks difficult to execute. And sail changes were exhausting. A task such as changing to a bigger spinnaker which might take 10 minutes in calm conditions, could take almost an hour here. To gybe the spinnaker was also a one-hour procedure. The crews had to be in perfect shape for this type of work.

Team News Corp remained the most southerly placed yacht. While Ross and Nick were confident they'd plotted the right course to become the new race leader, they didn't want the opposition to know how well they were going. Ross sent out the yacht's daily email to race headquarters that was very much a smokescreen: *I have kept questioning myself, is there more pressure down here? Is there a better angle here? Shall we dive north at pace, take the gain and fall in behind?* (For this race, each yacht's position on the race course was plotted by satellite, but under race rules — for media purposes — all crews were required to transmit daily email reports, photographs and video camera vision relating to life onboard.)

A few hours later it was obvious they were on a roll. It was time to tell everyone how well things were going in their part of the world.

Ross:

> *We're smoking … sitting on 18 knots and surfing to 28 knots. Now we have a fractional spinnaker on, one reef in the main [sail] in 34 knots from the west. Everything, including our toothbrushes, is stacked at the back of the boat to keep the bow out of the water.*
>
> *Debating whether/when to peel [change] to the storm spinnaker. It's warmer on deck with the wind being out of the west instead of off the ice in the south. We're loving it. It is great sailing and we're hoping that we're continuing to put miles on the fleet.*
>
> *The boat is behaving fantastically — our helmsmen, Gordon Maguire, Steve Cotton, Barney Walker and Jeff Scott, who have all steered other Volvo Ocean 60 boats down here in previous races, are raving about how this boat handles — bow up, well balanced and accelerates easily.*
>
> *On a lighter note, having two Irishmen onboard is a struggle. Justin Slattery and Gordon both claim that they are the rugby world champions now. Their reasoning is England beat Australia, Ireland beat England and Australia were the world champions.*

Good helmsmen are vital in the Southern Ocean and *Team News Corp* was strong in this department. Steve Cotton and Jeff Scott, who were part of the team almost from the outset, were designated as the two watch leaders. Maguire and Ian 'Barney' Walker were welcome additions to the helming department.

Despite being an excellent helmsman, the Southern Ocean leg was the one aspect of the race that Steve liked least: 'I don't like the cold. People who say they do are bullshitting. I hear them all the time, saying, "It's the best sailing." Let me tell you, it's good for about nine hours, all very fun, and then you want to get out. While I don't have any fear of it, I just don't enjoy it. If anything, I'm probably more conscious of the boat than others down there. I listen to all the noises; I think about what might break.'

On the flipside, this is Scotty's view of the Southern Ocean: 'Speed. That's what it's all about. To put it into perspective, it's like a surfing contest; but comparing the first leg with the Southern Ocean leg is like comparing surfing in Sydney with surfing the monsters in Hawaii. It's fantastic just going down there and taking it on. It teaches you a lot about yourself. You have to go into yourself and control your own fear. I actually enjoy it, being on the edge. It's 99 per cent risk.'

Scotty certainly knew about risk — he's been over the side once, and was lucky to live through it. 'It was in the Southern Ocean when I was racing aboard *Yamaha*. I was down in the nav. station doing some work when I heard the stamp on the deck above my head, meaning, "Get up here right now — we need help." I rushed on deck without a safety harness. Next thing, a big wave hit us. It washed over the deck, picked me up and sent me sliding on my backside right across the cabin roof and out through the bottom lifeline. Somehow I grabbed a jib sheet [rope] as I went; so there I was, outside the boat, hanging onto the sheet and flapping along like a fish on a line. I don't know how I did it, but I managed to hold on and eventually pull myself back aboard the boat.'

Having come up through the ranks, Scotty appreciates just how dangerous it is for the foredeck crew in rugged conditions: 'It's really hard on those guys. When it's time to crack [set] a storm chute [spinnaker] they get it set up, then sit on deck waiting for it to burst open; waiting to make sure everything's OK. The next thing, it pops and you go from 10 knots to 25 knots in a flash. The whole boat just spears underwater as it accelerates.

That's when those guys are at their highest risk up the front. It's my job at the back to keep them safe.'

Safe! This stage of the leg was close to being very unsafe. It was where these crews were really earning their keep. It was becoming one of the wildest and wettest rollercoaster rides on the planet.

Ross:

Day 8 — We're flying, under and over water. We sailed 120 miles in six hours and if we can maintain this it will be 480 miles in 24 hours! A world record...

We have 30–40 knots, huge, rolling seas and we're surfing up to 28 knots. All we have to do is keep it together and not crash and burn. Believe me, it is a high-stress environment. Five guys on deck: one driving, with the spinnaker trimmer and main trimmer sitting right aft, while the two grinders are in the main cockpit. The off watch are sleeping in their wet-weather gear as far aft as possible waiting for the call to 'Get it off' — that means 'Get the spinnaker off, in a real hurry.' There are a few other adjectives added to this, which I can't repeat.

We are sailing the fine line, but the gains are huge. We have been like this for eight hours and should maintain the pressure for another six, then it will lighten.

After driving for two hours Barney Walker has just come down and announced: 'The boat's bloody incredible — never driven anything like it in my life.' High praise from the Aussie.

...Time for me to get back on deck. We've just started to head north, and when I announced it, it was like the crew had just won Lotto.

Gundy:

Crazy, crazy times out here. Just got down below after four hours of hair-raising sailing. In four hours we did somewhere around 50 miles — and I lost a bunch of hair for every single one! The good news is that the boat, sail and crew are all still in one piece and, actually, we are in great shape.

It's been really cold; I am typing still wearing my survival suit. On each watch my feet and hands have been going numb in the first hour on deck. Yesterday was a bad day for sleep, with lots of [spinnaker] peels. Today promises to be the same. At least it all gets us to Sydney quickly! Thank God we have four of the best helmsmen in the fleet onboard; Barney, Steve, Scotty and Gordon are awesome — keeping us up the right way.

For me now, it's a few hours' sleep in wet kit, then back into the cold for another dose of adrenaline!

RECORD! The great news came for the *Team News Corp* crew late on 18 November. The blue and white rocket had been sailed over a distance of 450.13 nautical miles in 24 hours: an average speed of 18.754 knots. Ironically, the record was taken from British yacht *Silk Cut* in the previous race, when Jez was a crewmember. The bonus was that *Team News Corp*, in being well to the south, was skirting around the rest of the fleet to the north and would soon take the lead.

Ross:

Broke the 24-hour record. Fantastic. It was bloody hard work, but very rewarding. The best part was that we pulled heaps of miles out of the opposition and are still pushing to take the lead. I believe we are still placed very well to take the lead within the next 48 hours.

The last 24 hours of sailing was right on the edge. We had the right boat, great sail combinations, excellent crew work and the best weather to wring the hell out of the boat. We had a west/northwest wind at 30 to 40 knots and huge, rolling seas so that we could maintain speeds well over 20 knots. The waves were big enough for us to surf down without nosediving; she didn't just hit the bottom and keep going. She was pounding down the waves, giving off that nice sound, boom, boom, boom, boom, down the waves. We had the storm chute up and two reefs in the main. All the guys were stacked down at the back of the boat, as was everything inside. Everyone below deck was living and sleeping at the back.

If the weather had continued, I am sure we would have had a 460- or even a 480-mile run. Above all, we didn't make any mistakes.

Right now, the winds have moderated and we're reaching in 25 knots, making good time towards the bottom of Australia. We'll definitely be having a beer to celebrate the record when we get to Sydney.

Shreda:

The record run was quite unbelievable. I remember looking behind the boat at one stage and couldn't believe my eyes. We had a 1.5-metre-high rooster tail coming off the transom and our wake was just disappearing in the wave after wave behind us. Each time a big wave came along it would just pick us up and blast us down its face — off we'd go again, surfing, 20, 24, 25 knots. Bloody exciting. Then I'd turn around, look towards the bow and ask myself, 'Why the hell am I bowman? There's no way I want to go forward of the mast in this ... it's wet, it's wild and we're just going too fast.'

I must say, though, that when the call came from the nav. station saying we'd just broken the 24-hour record, that was just wicked. Morale on the boat soared through the roof.

It was no different on other boats. Crew safety was paramount, as was the security of the boat, but no matter how hard the wind was blowing, how cold it was or how big the seas were, sails had to be changed. This was when things became dangerous.

Knut Frostad — skipper, *djuice dragons*:

Right now, we have 44 knots of wind over the deck. We just finished a headsail change. Changing headsails in more than 40 knots is probably the most difficult and dangerous change we have — six guys hooked on with safety lines on the bow, trying to pull the old jib down and inboard. The boat is still logging up to 20 knots and suddenly a wave washes the bow, pushing the six big guys back at high speed. Then they crawl forward and start pulling the jib in all over again. Soaking wet but still smiling, we eventually crawl back together into the cockpit.

If this isn't mad, then what is?

While the wind was going soft in the south it was holding for the yachts in the north, and it soon became obvious that *Team News Corp*'s lead would be short-lived. So would their world record. On the day that the *Team SEB* crew would refer to as 'Big Tuesday', they blew away *Team News Corp*'s record. The new mark was 460.4 nautical miles: a remarkable effort for a VO 60-class yacht, and just seven miles off the outright world record for a single-hulled yacht. The top speed the *SEB* team saw during this rocketship ride was a staggering 34.7 knots.

The race for first into Sydney remained as close as ever; in fact, it was almost too close at one stage.

Mark Rudiger — navigator, *ASSA ABLOY*:

We were screaming along in the Roaring Forties when we had to change from the small spinnaker to a headsail. We must have shortly thereafter run into a patch of weed, because [the boat was going noticeably slower]. By then it was pitch-black and blowing up to 35 … and Neal McDonald convinced us that we needed to get the weed off. So we dropped the headsail [and started sailing the boat backwards] while we all looked over the side to see if the weed was coming off.

'LOOK OUT, THERE'S ANOTHER BOAT!'

illbruck went screaming right past us like a runaway train in the middle of the night. We don't know which of us was more surprised!

The cold in these climes influenced everything the sailors did. While their yachts were careering across the ocean at breakneck speeds the crews found that when compared with sailing in the tropics they were operating in slow motion. The cold even made the catering a more burdensome task.

Ross:

Day 9 — Cooking down south is a major exercise. We have this little gas burner with small screw-in bottles — the biggest problem is that the cold weather causes the gas to burn without much heat. It's like trying to heat a saucepan of water at home using a match. Heating the water to add to the freeze-dried food takes an hour and then it cools down so quickly. It's around 5–8 degrees C inside the boat, except for the hour in which we have a little diesel heater cranked up. The temp. then gets up to a magical 10–12 degrees C.

One way to have the food hold its 'heat' was to serve chilli …

Jez:

Day 10 — Just enjoyed a very nice chilli in a relatively stable boat for the first time in three days … three days spent on a 24-hour rollercoaster ride whilst being hosed down with cold water that sometimes had the force to knock you off your perch, resulting in a fair amount of bruised bodies. Steering has been with the aid of goggles to try to give you some chance of seeing ahead as the boat hurtles through waves at 22 knots.

First five boats within 30 miles of each other so we have a yacht race on our hands as we head towards Eclipse Island (off the southwestern corner of Australia) 1400 miles away.

On Day 11 it was revealed that a life-threatening drama was developing aboard *Amer Sports One*. Roger Nilson, the onboard doctor, sent a message to race headquarters reporting that their sail trimmer, Keith Kilpatrick, was sick with a stomach illness. Grant Dalton and his crew were in sixth place, approximately 1500 nautical miles southwest of Australia. The race officials alerted the Australian Maritime Rescue Co-ordination Centre.

Suffering from a suspected blocked intestine, Keith was being treated with antibiotics and morphine, but the boat's medical supplies were running low. The Royal Australian Airforce sent a P3 Orion, a plane that had been used successfully on previous rescue situations, to drop the required medical supplies. This went without a hitch and when *Amer Sports One* reached Eclipse Island, Keith was taken to hospital. He was able to make it to Sydney to welcome the yacht but, on the advice of doctors, he quit the race.

With the lead yachts starting to make a positive course change to the northeast and towards the Australian mainland, the crews could have been forgiven for thinking the worst was behind them. But that wasn't to be the case. Their boats and bodies would still experience plenty of punishment before they saw Sydney.

Ross:

Day 12 — What incredible racing. After blasting through the Southern Ocean for 3000-odd miles, damaging our boats and bodies, dodging icebergs, and

Top *ASSA ABLOY* becomes a surfboat as it thunders up the east coast of Australia towards Sydney.

Centre The bowman on *Amer Sports One* works on releasing the spinnaker from the end of the spinnaker pole while the yacht charges towards Sydney.

Bottom Knockdown. A spectacular rather than grand entrance to Sydney for *Amer Sports One* — the end result of the yacht going out of control soon after the photo in the middle of the page was taken.

All images *Rick Tomlinson*

Top Sydney's Opera House marks the finishing line for *illbruck* as it leads the fleet home at the end of Leg Two. *Rick Tomlinson*

Bottom A welcome sight. *Team News Corp* sails into its home port, Sydney, in third place, making it two out of two podium finishes. *Richard Langdon/Ocean Images*

Top left The chief executive of the VOR, Helge Alten, greets a bearded Jez and friend in Sydney.

Top right Jez heads the line-up of skippers at the welcome ceremony conducted by an Aboriginal elder in Sydney.

Centre left Spencer Moseska, vice-president of News Corp Marketing, gets a feel for VO 60 sailing on Sydney Harbour. He coordinated the project for the company.

Centre right Not just sailors. *Team News Corp*'s Jez Fanstone and Oli Allard were part of a rock group comprising members of various syndicates that entertained in Sydney.

Below left Santa Claus — looking very much like Jez in a beard and red suit — arrived for the team's Christmas Day lunch in Sydney.

Below right What a day! Bart struggles to cope with Christmas Day Down Under.

All images *Richard Langdon/Ocean Images*

Top Fireworks explode from the top of city buildings as part of the trophy presentation ceremony in Sydney.

Bottom left Bart Simpson's trip around the world with *Team News Corp* saw him visit many of the world's best-known tourist attractions.

Bottom right *Team News Corp*'s co-skipper Ross Field places a wreath on the waters of Sydney Harbour in memory of Sir Peter Blake, a former winner of the Volvo race and a man considered to be one of the world's greatest offshore sailors.

Right Bridge climbers. Two of the *Team News Corp* crew tend the mainsail as the yacht moves under the Sydney Harbour Bridge.

Top *Team News Corp* in pre-start manoeuvres with *illbruck* prior to the start of the Sydney to Hobart to Auckland leg.

Bottom In an atmosphere filled with smoke from raging bushfires, *Team News Corp* leads the VOR and Sydney to Hobart race fleets away from Sydney at the start of Leg Three.

All images *Rick Tomlinson*

Top left Nature unleashed all its fury just south of Sydney with this massive waterspout that menaced the VOR fleet. The picture, taken from the deck of *Team News Corp*, shows *ASSA ABLOY* in the distance. *Team News Corp*

Top right Lisa McDonald's crew guide *Amer Sports Too* towards Auckland. *Carlo Borlenghi, Sea & See*

Centre left *Team News Corp* relishing the rough going while heading to Hobart. *Rick Tomlinson*

Bottom *illbruck* making haste into Auckland. The German entry's winning streak ended here. *Daniel Forster, illbruck*

Top left Exhausted. *Team News Corp* watch leader Gordon Maguire shows the strain after four exhausting hours sailing the yacht through the Southern Ocean ice fields. After just four hours in their bunks, he and his team would be back on deck again. *Team News Corp*

Top right How cold does it get in the Southern Ocean? Cold enough for snow, as is revealed on *illbruck*'s deck. *Ray Davies*

Bottom Chilled out. Knut Frostad (*third from left*) and *djuice dragons* crewmembers leave no doubt about the size of some of the icebergs they were confronted by in the Southern Ocean. *djuice dragons*

taking many different tactical options, here are five boats within 20 miles of each other. We sighted ASSA ABLOY and djuice today.

Scotty and I are recovering from back injuries we suffered two days ago when we were thrown from the wheel of the boat by a huge wave in two separate incidents. I have cracked ribs and heavy bruising to my back and Scotty has suspected bruised kidneys. The power of the wave that hit me was amazing — it completely flattened me. Luckily, Barney saw what was happening and leapt to the wheel as the boat was charging along at 20 knots with no one steering.

Ross broke his ribs because of the pressure exerted on his chest by his safety harness. The wave ripped him away from the wheel, and his rapid exit towards the back of the boat was brought to an abrupt halt by his harness strop. These were the sorts of injuries you have to take in your stride in a race like this.

Ross:

Day 14 — There are now four boats within five miles of each other. We have made gains, but had a disaster when we blew out the reaching spinnaker that had given us such great boat speed.

Right now, Alby and Jez are down below fixing the spinnaker, which is going to take eight hours. Here's hoping we don't need it in the near future.

We have SEB 0.753 miles behind, but we are now holding. Our plan is to be in contact at Eclipse Island 423 miles away so we are on a level playing field for the 1800 miles to Sydney.

Scotty's and my injuries are feeling better. The painkillers are disappearing fast but I'm sure we'll have enough for the next eight to nine days.

When you're the onboard sailmaker the last thing you want to see is a blown-out spinnaker, especially when you're in the Southern Ocean ...

Alby:

I was in my bunk and I could feel the boat going. I knew it was going to broach [turn side-on to the wind and be knocked flat]. I just grabbed the side of my bunk, hung on, and hoped. I could hear the spinnaker flapping as the boat went over and I was saying, 'Please don't blow out; don't blow out.' When I heard all the swearing I knew it was gone. You just feel this hollow thing in the bottom of your stomach: 'Oh man, back to the sewing machine.' The competitive side of me hopes it is all there; that the guys recover all the bits so it can be repaired, but the other side says, 'Oh, if it's missing a massive bit I don't need to fix it.' This one we had to fix.

Eclipse Island, a tiny rocky outcrop that barely pops through the surface of the ocean, was a rounding mark for the fleet on this leg. The approach to the island was in direct contrast to conditions down south. The wind became very light and the fleet compressed. *Amer Sports One* brought breeze up from behind and rejoined the race.

The considerably slower pace provided time to reflect on what had happened over the previous two weeks ...

Stu Bannatyne — watch leader, *illbruck*:

Well, the Southern Ocean feels like it has truly gone now as we sit here, becalmed, almost in sight of Australia. The boots are coming off and layers of thermals and socks are being peeled off carefully to reveal white limbs and soggy feet. Some guys have not seen their bodies since start day and are quite relieved that they have at least some semblance of muscle tone, although we're not the Arnold Schwarzeneggers we once were.

Time to reflect quickly on a harsh but typical passage through the Southern Ocean. We saw 'bergs on the third day, a little earlier than expected, but spectacular nevertheless and a reminder of how nature will do as she pleases. One of the main drawcards of this race for me is the adrenaline-pumping, hang-onto-the-edge-of-your-seat, Southern Ocean sleigh ride of heavy air downwind sailing. We had a small taste and the buzz was definitely still there. However, after a few days of rather more unpleasant blast reaching [power sailing across the wind direction in heavy conditions] I think in future I will be looking for my adrenaline rush somewhere other than 50 degrees south. Perhaps skydiving or windsurfing in Hawaii might do the trick. Previously I have said that the good times always outweighed the bad when it came to the Southern Ocean, but that was usually with a few years to forget the low times. With the memory only slightly blurred I think I may be turning … DO NOT DELETE THIS MESSAGE and please show it to me if I start talking about sailing another Volvo Ocean Race.

With virtually no wind and a gentle swell running, the race yachts were being rocked from side to side, waddling like ducks ever so slowly towards the island. Already red and burning from the saltwater blasting they had copped a few days earlier, the crews' eyes were now trying to focus on anything that looked like the slightest puff of wind ruffling the ocean surface. A puff could make all the difference. *Team SEB* found one … a puff that came via legend …

Gareth Cooke — trimmer, *Team SEB*:
Myth and legend has it that the albatross is a friend, companion and partner of the mariner. Yesterday we may have been witness to the myth.

On a glassy, calm sea, even the slightest hint of a breeze was discussed and analysed as to its usefulness to our cause. A seemingly hopeless, tiny little puff of wind was noticed, discussed and eventually written off as being too small to make a difference. Our helmsman at the time, Tony Mutter, suggested the harmless zephyr was not, in fact, a puff of wind, but an albatross's fart!

Albatross fart or not, this little breeze filled our drifter [lightweight headsail] and helped us to the next puff which, in turn, assisted us to the next, and so it went until we were in a steady breeze, with illbruck and Co slowly disappearing behind.

The next sked revealed the albatross had assisted us to a 13-mile lead. Now around Eclipse Island in first place, we are extremely grateful to the albatross that farted next to our boat and are working hard to maintain the lead over the chasing pack.

The assistance from the 'albatross' was enough to get *SEB* past Eclipse Island at 4am (GMT) on Day 17. Their navigator, Marcel van Triest, left the yacht as it rounded the island to fly home to Sweden following the death of a family member. *Team News Corp* rounded two hours later in fourth place behind *illbruck* (four miles ahead) and *ASSA ABLOY* (one mile ahead). *djuice* was fifth and *Amer Sports One* sixth. The fleet was lining up for a great battle to the finish some 1800 miles away.

Ross:

Day 19 — Reaching again, spray, solid water, chilly, but at least the sun is out and we're making good miles direct at the mark (Bass Strait — between the Australian mainland and Tasmania).

Note: No one on board has washed themselves since the start of this leg and we're all wearing the same clothes. Thank goodness for all the polypropylene and quick-dry clothing we have now. The old cotton T-shirts and wool are definitely a thing of the past.

Day 20 — Sorry, made a mistake in the last report ... some of the guys have washed! Don't know how, when or where, because there isn't any warm water, soap (at least there shouldn't be), towels, or anything you would associate with a wash onboard. Anyway, I'm sure I'm not the only one who is dirty.

Nick:

Day 20 — We are now less than 1000 miles from Sydney. The leg is not yet won or lost, but I have been reflecting on the past couple of weeks. What makes people want to do this race and how does it change them? For some, like myself, it is the challenge and adventure, while for others it may be part of their sailing career.

Most of us avoid the publicity an event like this generates, whereas some love the public attention. This race subjects you to an extreme change of environment: from space, mobility, cleanliness, good food and varied companionship to cold and cramped conditions, and unwholesome food with the same 11 people for weeks on end. It brings out the best and worst in people and you are never the same again.

I have been through the biggest lows and highs of my life this year and will forever have a different and, I think, better outlook on life and the world around me. I have made friends I will always remember; maybe that is the most important thing of all.

A weather change soon moved across the Great Australian Bight and turned a near-drifting race into a power-packed spinnaker run towards Bass Strait. It was wet and wild — shades of the Southern Ocean, only warmer. *Team News Corp* was still managing to hold down third place, having passed

ASSA ABLOY. During that last night before entering Bass Strait there was high drama onboard ...

Ross:

> Gordon told me the initial part of the story because I was asleep in my bunk. Scotty has four false front teeth and when he steers the boat he always has his tongue hanging out, constantly flicking his teeth in and out of place. I guess it's all part of him concentrating. It was blowing dogs off chains this particular night and Scotty, who was steering, was trying to talk to Nick on the intercom between the cockpit and the nav. station below. He was yelling so hard, trying to be heard over all the noise associated with the boat going so fast, that he literally blew his teeth out. All you heard then was, 'Crytht, cor, I've lotht my fuckin' teef.' So here we are in the middle of this high-level competition and Scotty has all the crew crawling around the back of the cockpit with torches, trying to find his false teeth. The first I knew about it was when Scotty came below, shook me in my bunk and woke me up. 'Roth, Roth,' he shouted. I shot bolt upright, wide awake immediately, thinking the rig must have fallen out.
>
> 'Fuck, what's wrong, Scotty,' I asked, trying to gather my senses.
>
> 'Roth, I've lotht my fuckin' teef,' he said.
>
> We mounted another search for the missing teeth when daylight came, but they couldn't be found; so I guess some crayfish off King Island is wearing them. It was tough on everyone after that. Scotty is hard to understand at the best of times because he mumbles. Without his teeth it was impossible. We told him he wasn't allowed to smile for the cameras when we got to Sydney because he looked so awful.

Although *News Corp* was the first-ever Australian entry in this event and now sailing in home waters, the welcome mat was yet to come out.

Ross:

> *Day 21 — Night time: broached, then rolled her out in a puff of 38 knots while carrying masthead spinnaker and a full main. The poor old boat lay on her side, flapping and screaming, and then the spinnaker fell apart. The guys got her back upright, pulled the spinnaker down, threw it in the bilge and we took off again doing 20 knots under main only. Got the fractional [non-masthead] spinnaker on and were off again within 15 minutes.*
>
> *We have suffered and lost 10 miles straight away and a further five miles being underpowered. As one crewmember said, a broach costs 10 miles and $100 000 — a slight exaggeration, but it's expensive in every sense of the word.*
>
> *Needless to say the language wasn't that great, but these things happen when you are pushing the boat 120 per cent the whole time. Alby looked at the spinnaker in the bilge, made a statement about its state (can't repeat), then got stuck in and repaired it. Ten hours later, it was back up and we're under full steam. Another incredible repair. I don't know how he does it. I would have binned it . . .*
>
> *We have ASSA ABLOY in sight to leeward, running under spinnaker. She's always hanging around us.*

Team SEB was another boat to crash and burn in these conditions. However, their experience was far more expensive; it cost them the lead.

Until that moment the Swedes looked set for first, but they pressed too hard. The spinnaker should have been replaced with a smaller one when the wind topped 28 knots, but they decided to hang onto it because they were continuing to open out on *illbruck*. But then the wind went to 34, 36, 38, then 40 knots! The inevitable happened.

Gurra Krantz — *SEB*:

Last night was one of those nights we will never forget. One reason is that we had a masthead chute up in 40 knots and enormous waves ... we wiped out and shattered the spinnaker. One wave was bigger than the others and in combination with an extra gust we just spun out ... on the side, in a wild broach, the big spinnaker flogging wildly, shaking the whole boat and making the very strong carbon [fibre] mast look like spaghetti. We couldn't get the boat back under control in the waves and we were forced to look at the chute being torn to pieces as we were taking it down.

More problems followed immediately ... one sheet went under the boat and jammed the rudder. Presumably illbruck *was on track doing 20 knots.*

That was the case. While *SEB* crewman Tom Braidwood had to dive overboard and swim under the boat to clear the line from the rudder, *illbruck* maintained its charge and went to the front. *SEB* lost more than 30 minutes due to the wipeout, which equates to 10 miles or more in those conditions.

The *illbruck* crew were more than pleased to learn at the next sked that they'd passed it. But as mastman Jamie Gale explained, there was still plenty of pain onboard, a legacy of the Southern Ocean: 'It is still cold ... and the old body is starting to seize up, especially the hands. This morning I found them fixed in a claw-like position and so stiff that I couldn't move them without hooking them onto something and gently straightening them out one by one. Painful? You'd better believe it. It's a pretty common affliction onboard for anyone who hangs onto a wheel, sheet or grinder handle, and that's most of us. Will there be any long-term effects? You can bet on it.'

BASS STRAIT IS a relatively shallow stretch of water that has claimed hundreds of vessels over the centuries. It was certainly not on its best behaviour for the Volvo boats. Approaching the northwestern corner of Tasmania, the leading yachts opted to sail to the south of King Island, except for *ASSA ABLOY* which, until then, had been pressuring *Team News Corp* for third. It was a grave error of judgment. *ASSA* found a far less favourable wind pattern and saw what might have been a third place convert into a sixth.

Jez:

> Day 21 — As we approach the infamous Bass Strait, we are expecting southeasterlies rising to 35 knots. Knowing this place, it will blow a zillion times more than that. All the reef lines have been put in, the harnesses are ready to go and the hatches are ready to be battened.
>
> We are ready for one last beating before we reach Sydney, 500 miles away.

Ross:

> Day 23 — SEB is just ahead of us, and we're comfortably locked into third place. We have a few tricks up our sleeves and some tactics planned to have a go at SEB and illbruck as we come up the coast. We've been reaching in very heavy south-east winds and there has been water everywhere. It's been shocking — we've been bailing 24 hours a day. As we round the corner, winds have settled and we'll be hoisting the spinnaker for the final run to Sydney.

The home-straight run to the finish turned into an exhilarating surf up the east coast under masthead spinnaker.

Shreda:

> Because we could see land I actually found it more exciting in some ways than when we broke the world

record in the Southern Ocean. Even though we weren't doing quite the same speeds, we were sailing past points of reference, so I could really relate to how fast we were going — like, 'There goes Nowra. There goes Jervis Bay. Here comes Wollongong.' It was a fantastic way to finish the leg.

Sydney showed why it's one of the most beautiful ports in the world when first *illbruck*, then *SEB* and *Team News Corp*, entered the harbour and made the final dash to the finish line, which was set immediately adjacent to one of the world's most identifiable buildings, the Sydney Opera House. A fleet of spectator and media vessels escorted them from the harbour entrance to the line.

While *illbruck* had consolidated its points advantage with two leg wins, *Team News Corp* had moved into a very satisfying second overall. Ross looked back on the leg with Jez and decided that more changes needed to be made. Strengthening the team as they went was part of their pre-race philosophy.

Ross:

I think we got this leg right about 80 per cent of the time, and we proved again that we are a fast boat. We proved that we are sailing the boat correctly.

We had a few crew issues, which we have now addressed. The big move is that Gordon Maguire has agreed to join us full-time and replace Steve as the watch leader. He's a very talented sailor and the guys really like him. He's a natural leader of men; he's a motivator who can draw the best out of people. One of the guys described him as being 'as smooth as polished dog shit'. It's a compliment. He's a bloody good bloke. Steve is no longer a watch leader; he is coming to sit on the nav. station with me — he will be more involved in the boat-to-boat tactical stuff, because that's where we need strengthening. Nick is stepping ashore; he won't be sailing on the next leg because right now his head is not into the racing. Peter Isler will be coming aboard to work on the tactics.

We learnt one very important thing about the boat on this leg: every other time we've raced these boats around the world and the wind has been very light we've experimented with leeward ballast — stacking everything to leeward and heeling the boat over. It's never worked — but this time it did. I guess this new design suits it. Coming into King Island we used it, and we were off like a rocket. Quite unbelievable.

Overall, I think Jez and I have the program together well. Things are going according to plan. We've kept the focus well and we're easing up a little bit on the budget. The money's there now to hire an additional person for the shore crew to take some of the load off the sailing team.

There's no doubt we can win this race. Only two of nine legs are gone and we're second on points.

With two wins bringing *illbruck* a total of 16 points (eight points for first on each leg, seven points for second, and so on) the German entry held a comfortable lead over *Team News Corp* on 12, *Amer Sports One* 11 and *SEB* 10. A yacht that failed to complete a stage received points for last place, i.e. one point, so *Tyco* was languishing on six points, three ahead of *Amer Sports Too*, which had recorded a last and second last on the two legs.

< Not gone with the wind! The bulk of the fleet barely make headway on Sydney Harbour at the start of Leg Three.

Rick Tomlinson

>> # SYDNEY TO HOBART TO AUCKLAND

Yacht racing is a cruel beast to play with.

JEZ FANSTONE

You didn't need to listen to the radio news or read the newspapers to know that Sydney was facing a horrendous natural disaster on Boxing Day, 26 December, the day that Leg Three of the Volvo Ocean Race was to start. The air was thick with a sepia-coloured smoke that made a Los Angeles smog look good; and there was a distinct smell of burnt eucalypt trees.

The source of the smoke was a series of massive bushfires that had broken out on Christmas Day and were ringing the city. Within 48 hours more than 110 homes would be lost and tens of thousands of acres of bushland burnt out.

Christmas Day had started as a 'brochure day' — clear blue skies with a forecast temperature of 28 degrees C. But by early afternoon a hot northwesterly wind was howling across the city and creating tinderbox conditions. In a very short time, Sydney looked like it was being bombed, with palls of smoke rising from many parts of the metropolitan area.

As it was high summer, many crews went for a swim on Christmas Day at one of the city's many surf beaches. Others celebrated Christmas lunch at harbourside restaurants; the *SEB* team even went to the extreme of buying a load of snow from a local ice-skating rink to create a Scandinavian atmosphere for their celebration. The *News Corp* team — 40 sailors, shore crew, wives, partners, family and friends — opted to escape the city precincts and celebrate at a supporter's home overlooking Pittwater, a beautiful tree-lined waterway on Sydney's northern beaches. A wonderful day full of Christmas spirit and great camaraderie was capped off with the arrival of Santa Claus, complete with a sack full of gifts for everyone present. As always with Christmas, the best part was watching the children open their surprise packages. Excitement prevailed. But Santa's true identity was almost blown when one youngster pointed at his feet and very loudly demanded to know: 'Why are you wearing Jez's sandals?'

As festive as it was, though, the pressure of the next leg weighed on everyone's mind. Before the start in Southampton it was freely tipped that Leg Three could provide an insurmountable hurdle for some yachts.

Jez:

> *The countdown to the start is with you from a week out. It might have been Christmas week, but you don't have a Christmas, you don't have a Christmas spirit; you spend the week getting the boat ready rather than going to the pub, meeting up with your mates and celebrating. And then Christmas Day is unique because you know that the next day you're going to be racing, so it's hard to relax. It was all very much in the back of my mind. It was a fantastic day that was very much a family celebration, but you could still sense a bit of tension in the air — everyone felt it because they knew what they were going into the next day.*

There was a unique aspect about Leg Three. It was a smidgen over 2000 miles from Sydney to Auckland, but it would include one of the world's classic ocean races, the 630-mile Sydney to Hobart yacht race, as part of it. And in a world first, the yachts would make a mandatory three-and-a-half-hour 'pit stop' before continuing on to Auckland. The merit of such a stopover was hotly debated before the start. For the sponsors it was a way of generating media interest in the race, while for the sailors it was seen as more of an imposition than anything else. Most decided to see how it went before voicing a final opinion on the effectiveness of the stop-go procedure.

Each year, hundreds of thousands of Sydneysiders line the shores of the harbour, sit on the decks of harbourside homes and apartments, or cram onto more than 1000 boats to watch the start of the Hobart race. Millions more follow the action via a two-hour live national telecast. Sailors consider this race to be one of the world's ultimate offshore challenges, and one of the most dangerous; which was never more evident than in the 1998 race when what could only be described as a cyclone ripped through the fleet, taking with it six lives. Five yachts sank while heroic paramedics and helicopter crews winched 55 sailors to safety. The wind topped 80 knots and there is photographic proof that the waves were at times more than 80 feet high.

The Sydney to Hobart yacht race had particularly poignant memories for Jez. He competed in that tragic 1998 race and lost a very close friend, Englishman Glyn Charles, who went overboard from the yacht *Sword of Orion* when it was rolled 360 degrees by a monstrous wave. The force snapped Charles's safety harness. His body was never found.

Jez:

> *The Hobart race is a very emotional thing for me. The 1998 race is something I'd rather not talk about. All I can say is that I've done two Hobarts and they've been the most miserable sails of my life. For sure, I'm looking forward to it this time as part of the Volvo Ocean Race, but it doesn't hold happy memories for me.*

Ross had a similar lack of enthusiasm for the race: 'No, I'm not looking forward to it. It's almost inevitable that when you leave here you'll be slammed by a bloody southerly buster [southerly gale]. You just belt your brains out and bash your body for a day or so, then you're into Hobart. The only consolation is that I know we can win this leg — we're fast upwind — but I'm not going to slit my wrists if we come third. But we don't want a third; we want to win it.'

Fortunately, there was an alternative view. *Team News Corp* helmsman Barney Walker was a helmsman aboard the VO 60, *Nokia*, two years earlier when it set the record time for the race: a stunning 19 hours for the 630 miles. For Barney the race was a memorable downhill slide: loaded to the gunwales with exhilaration.

For Leg Three, the departure of the teams from the dock outside the National Maritime Museum on Sydney Harbour was in direct contrast to the energetic and colourful scenes in Southampton and Cape Town. The mood was sombre for a very good reason. During the stopover, the Volvo race crews were shattered to learn that Sir Peter Blake — one of the world's greatest offshore racing sailors and a man who had no peer in this round-the-world race — had been murdered by pirates aboard his yacht during an environmental expedition along the Amazon River. He had had an impact

Top After surviving a near-catastrophic knockdown and dismasting in the Southern Ocean, *SEB* was jury-rigged and sailed 1250 nautical miles to safety at Cape Horn. A spinnaker pole was used as a mast. *Rick Tomlinson*

Bottom Ross Field sits on the cockpit floor to steer *Team News Corp* very slowly into Rio de Janeiro. The emergency rudder can be seen attached to the stern of the yacht. *Richard Langdon/Ocean Images*

Top Sleeping below deck on *Team News Corp* in warm weather. It's the bedroom, bathroom, kitchen, storage room and workshop all in one. *Richard Langdon/Ocean Images*

Bottom left *djuice*'s resident nudist, Anthony 'Nocka' Nossiter, bares all while rounding Cape Horn. *djuice dragons*

Bottom right Home on a wing and a prayer. *Team News Corp*'s emergency rudder was continually reinforced during the 1200 nautical miles it was used to get the yacht to Rio. *Richard Langdon/Ocean Images*

Top The rudderless *Team News Corp* is hoisted from the water in Rio.

Bottom left Jez visits the massive Christ the Redeemer shrine that towers over Rio de Janeiro.

Bottom right From boat to bath. *Team News Corp*'s Damian 'Shreda' Duke cleans up in Rio after a month at sea.

All images *Richard Langdon/Ocean Images*

Top left Smooth is fast. Warwick 'Wazza' Kerr prepares to polish the underbody of *Team News Corp*'s hull. *Richard Langdon/Ocean Images*

Top right A punch in the nose for *SEB*. The bow damage was caused by its collision with *illbruck* after leaving Rio on Leg Five. *Rick Tomlinson*

Bottom The *Team News Corp* crew work on trimming the sails and 'cleaning house' soon after the start in Miami. *Richard Langdon/Ocean Images*

Right The McDonalds get it right. Lisa McDonald's *Amer Sports Too*, followed by husband Neal steering *ASSA ABLOY*, were the only two yachts given a clear start in Miami. *Rick Tomlinson*

Top left *Team News Corp*'s 'almost perfect' start off Miami. The five yachts in this photo, along with *illbruck*, were called back to start again after officials claimed they crossed the line before the gun. *Richard Langdon/Ocean Images*

Top right The golden glow of a Chesapeake Bay sunrise welcomes *Team News Corp* on what would be a golden day. Victory on Leg Six was just 120 miles away. *Rick Tomlinson*

Bottom Bart Simpson points very determinedly towards the finish line as *Team News Corp* nears Baltimore.

Richard Langdon/Ocean Images

Top The *Team News Corp* crew experience that winning feeling after arriving in Baltimore.
Richard Langdon/Ocean Images

Bottom left Jez throw's the opening pitch at a Baltimore Orioles baseball game in Baltimore. *Rick Tomlinson*

Bottom right Smiling in the rain. *Team News Corp*'s crew assembles on deck before the start out of Annapolis.
Richard Langdon/Ocean Images

Top left *Team News Corp*'s battle flag held the premier position when the fleet docked at the end of Leg Six.

Top right Gordon Maguire appears to be happy with the *Team News Corp*'s start as they set sail from Annapolis and head across the Atlantic to La Rochelle, France.

Bottom It's never too wet to go yacht racing. Four of the fleet sail under Annapolis' Bay Bridge following the wet and windy start of Leg Seven.

All images *Richard Langdon/Ocean Images*

on so many of the contestants in the Volvo race, including Ross, who had been his watch leader when *Steinlager* won all six legs of the 1989/90 contest. Sir Peter had competed five times and, beyond that, had been the driving force behind New Zealand's win and subsequent successful defence of the America's Cup.

Just away from the dock the eight yachts formed a semicircle, the crews paying tribute to the memories and legacies of Sir Peter by casting floral wreaths onto the water. The yachts then moved down harbour, under the Sydney Harbour Bridge and past the Opera House, before entering the starting area three miles inside the harbour entrance.

Sadly, the bushfire smoke stripped the usually spectacular Hobart race start of most of its colour. But it didn't stop the crowds from coming out. The hills, bays and beach areas that make this harbour a magnificent natural amphitheatre were scenes of picnics and parties, while on the water everything from canoes and surf skis to multi-million-dollar mega yachts lined the course from the start line to the Heads.

The Volvo race yachts had a separate starting line from the 67 other Hobart race yachts. It was to be the first time in living memory that the race started at a snail's pace. Because of the density of the smoke, the land was not warming enough to create a thermal effect and suck in the northeasterly sea breeze. Instead, the harbour was a near-windless no-man's-land, with the already faint southwesterly getting softer and softer, and the sea breeze not able to fill the void.

When the boom of the start cannon echoed across the harbour at 1pm it was racing in slow motion. The yachts on the western shore made the first move, ghosting along on the last gasp of the southwesterly breeze. *Tyco* was the standout while, to the east, *Team News Corp* was parked … until the sea breeze fanned in over the hills. The first puff saw the Code Zero headsail unfurled and slowly but surely the speed built. The crew had made a calculated gamble that the sea breeze would come in, a gamble that would pay off handsomely. Within a few minutes they were in front and already making it very obvious they would show the entire fleet the way out of the harbour. It was a great debut for Steve Cotton, in his new role as tactician, and short-course expert Peter Isler, the American who had come aboard for the leg in place of Nick White.

The water around the yacht turned white as a huge armada of spectator craft escorted the leader out to sea. By the time they reached the offshore turning mark and the bow turned south towards Hobart, the *News Corp* team was $10 000 richer — a prize from a race sponsor for being the first yacht out to sea. The crew quickly agreed that the money should go to Sydney's bushfire disaster relief fund, which had been established to help families who had lost their homes and businesses. Their gesture received high praise.

Jez:

> *Being first out of the harbour in Sydney was a huge thing to happen for us, especially considering we were flying the Australian flag. There were crowds cheering; it was like being at a footy match. You looked round, thinking, 'Christ, this is a yacht race!' It was an excellent feeling for all of us.*

Being in front was one thing; staying there was the challenge, a real challenge considering the variables posed by this first stage of the leg. The inevitable southerly change was forecast to arrive that evening; there was a strong southerly current offshore, but out there the water was rougher; and beyond it all the opposition had to be covered. All this and more was being pondered when, suddenly, just before dark, a danger loomed that no one could have imagined.

Jez:

> *We held a 2-mile lead, then the bloody breeze dropped and the fleet compressed again. All that hard work went to waste.*
>
> *It became a frustrating drifting match, so I went down below with Steve and Peter to check on the course. Suddenly Alby charged down the companionway, shouting, 'Put the radar on, put the radar on. There's a waterspout, a waterspout! We've got to see which way it's*

going!' I went up on deck to see this grey funnel spiralling out of a big black cloud and heading towards us. An enormous vertical column of water and wind about a quarter of a mile wide, it was travelling at about 40 miles an hour. One minute it looked like it was going to the right of us, then to the left, then straight at us.

Ross:

At first it was quite fascinating to see it develop, but then as it got bigger and bigger and started coming towards us, I began to get concerned. We didn't know what we could do to avoid it because it was on such an erratic path, and we certainly didn't know what would happen if it hit us. It was totally unpredictable. We had nowhere to go. You watch movies like Twister *and see cows being sucked up and thrown out by the bloody thing; that was the thought I had in my mind. The logical thing to do was to drop the mainsail, so I told the guys to do that. Barney was steering and doing his best to get around it, but really, we were at its mercy.*

The crew became anxious about the outcome if they were engulfed by what was a maritime tornado. The yacht was not very manoeuvrable, as there was 3.5 tonnes of equipment plus water ballast loaded on one side. A knockdown could have dire consequences.

Barney:

I was just thinking what a lovely afternoon of sailing it had been when I looked out to the west and saw this little funnel coming out of a distant cloud. I thought, 'This is a joke; this could be a bit of entertainment.' I looked back to the west a few minutes later and could only shout, 'Oh my God ... this is one of the biggest twisters I've ever seen!' The thing had grown in diameter by about four times and was charging towards us. We decided we should take it a little seriously, but there wasn't a lot we could do about it because the wind was just dragging us towards its centre. Once we realised we were going to be a part of this thing we dropped the mainsail. By this stage it had grown twice as big again. It was huge. It was a serious-looking thing — it was like the pictures you see of tornados in America. Exactly that.

I started making a plan about what I could hang on to if we went through the middle of the thing. I figured that if I put myself in through the spokes of the steering wheel, then I couldn't be sucked up off the deck.

The *Team News Corp* crew watched in awe as the 80-foot maxi yacht *Nicorette* was swallowed up by the twister just ahead of them. Despite having no sails set, it was knocked flat by the ferocity of the wind. Incredibly, no one was injured, but the mainsail, which was tied to the boom, was so badly shredded that it had to be replaced.

Would they be next? The jib was still set to retain some manoeuvrability, but it could be lowered in a trice. First *illbruck*, then *ASSA ABLOY* were confronted by this incredible force of nature. Miraculously they were spared — barely — the whirling, roaring grey funnel seeming to change its mind, putting *Team News Corp* in its sights. It began hunting them down, hurling spray up like grey dust. The *News Corp* crew were helpless; their destiny was out of their control and in the hands of a giant natural vacuum cleaner that had a wildly oscillating suction pipe a quarter of a mile wide. They knew their entire round-the-world race program might end right there. And as if watching its approach wasn't enough, the large digital numerals on the wind speed read-out said everything — 20, 30, 40, 50 knots and climbing . . .

The spray and the rain started to tell just how close it was. Back in the cockpit, while anxious eyes continued to monitor its progress, Barney did everything possible to guide the yacht around the twister's perimeter.

The wind screeched through the rig at more than 60 knots and *Team News Corp* began to lie over on its side. Suddenly, the twister changed course ever so slightly and roared down the port side of the yacht like an out-of-control locomotive, the outer edge being less than 100 metres away. Phew!

With the ugly ogre continuing on its capricious path to the east and the clearing atmosphere came relief and the good news. *Team News Corp* was unscathed and back to being number one in the fleet. Keeping the jib set while the others had dropped all their sails had paid a mighty dividend. It was time to get back to the race: time to get back to business.

Within a very short time they were pounding their way south into the teeth of a freshening southwesterly wind. The excitement of the start and dramas of the twister were quickly replaced with body-bashing. The Hobart race was living up to its reputation for being a rough one and, not surprisingly, the galley wasn't getting a lot of use. Seasickness was the norm as the yachts bucked and tossed and corkscrewed over waves that were large, steep and close together. It was very uncomfortable. This was tough sailing, even without the twister.

It was as good as it was bad, though. *Team News Corp* was again showing its prowess as an upwind yacht by holding the lead in Bass Strait from *ASSA ABLOY* and *illbruck*. And even more impressive was the fact that they were leading the entire Sydney to Hobart race fleet, including the maxis.

Peter and Steve were considering tactics for the all-important approach to Tasman Island, which was a couple of hundred miles away at the entrance to Storm Bay.

Ross:

> Day 2 — *It has been a busy, exhausting 36 hours since the start and it's only now that we have settled into some good sailing — reaching with a jib topsail and staysail in 16 knots. We're 222 miles out from Tasman Island.*
>
> *The decision on how to approach Tasman Island is varying through the fleet, with ASSA ABLOY and us opting for the rhumb line [direct course] and the others coming from the east. Who's right? We are ...*
>
> *Time will tell, but we're happy where we are.*
>
> *It is great having Peter Isler on board — he's helping*

us a great deal. Of course, we're missing Nick on this leg as we have had some majors on the electronics. Nick used to fix things quietly, while I am inclined to fix things with a hammer and lots of noise.

It has been a very, very rough leg, with all the crew seasick and it's only tonight that we had our first cooked meal. We can now settle into our routine, thank goodness.

Not too much damage so far: broken battens in the main, broken runner block, plus a few bruised and battered bodies — Gundy tore his fingernail off, Gordon bashed his knee, my back is playing up again and everyone's eyes need holding open.

At this stage the fleet was relatively closely bunched, except for the crew on *Amer Sports Too*. They were finding the conditions tough going.

The first big news of the leg (after the twister) came when one of the yachts was forced to retire. *Team SEB*'s rudder had been ripped out of the bottom of the hull following the failure of the lower bearing accommodating the rudderpost. The yacht was in the middle of Bass Strait. A considerable amount of water flooded the interior before the hole was plugged with a bucket and the watertight bulkhead sealed. They fitted their emergency rudder so they could sail back to the mainland. The plan was to make temporary repairs, then sail directly to Auckland.

The next casualty was *Amer Sports Too*. The crew somehow managed to keep the mast in their boat when, as a result of the constant pounding, the forestay broke. They changed course rapidly downwind and secured halyards from the mast to the bow, which saved the rig. And as if that wasn't enough, their rudder split when a shark swam under the boat and became wrapped around the blade. Undeterred, they pressed on towards Hobart.

Sailing down Tasmania's east coast, once again on this leg all the efforts of the *Team News Corp* crew would be wasted. Hughie, the sailor's wind god, was to decide who would be first into Hobart.

With the broad and bright beam of light from the Tasman Island lighthouse arcing across the ocean from the top of the sheer cliffs that towered hundreds of feet above them, at around 2am on the third night at sea, *Team News Corp* turned the corner and entered Storm Bay first. *illbruck* was almost alongside and *Tyco* wasn't far away. The bay, however, was to be a giant trap. To be called Storm Bay was an oxymoron on this day. The wind had evaporated, the water was glassy smooth and the blackness of the night was only broken by the faint red, green and white navigation lights of the race yachts. Entering the bay was like sailing into a giant parking lot in which the boom gate went up, you entered, parked and watched the others follow you in. The three leading yachts stayed there long enough for *ASSA ABLOY* and *Amer Sports One* to come from miles behind and join them in the drifting match. Even *Nicorette* turned up. At some stage during the drift everyone could claim to have been in front.

It was essentially a case of 'first in, last out'. While *Team News Corp* and *illbruck* hunted down-draughts along the shore directly beneath the stunning rock columns of Cape Raoul's 'Organ Pipes', *ASSA ABLOY* made a small diversion, turning some 90 degrees from course and making very slow progress to the south. After sailing just 200 yards they struck gold — the faintest of puffs of wind cascaded from the cliff tops and got them moving. Within 30 minutes they were gone, as was *Amer Sports One*.

Surrounded by more than 100 spectator and media boats, *ASSA ABLOY* sailed the 12 miles up the Derwent River to arrive at Hobart's waterfront at 9.46 am. Within 47 minutes the first six yachts in the Volvo race fleet were home — the closest finish ever for the frontrunners in the 57-year history of the classic. The order was *ASSA ABLOY, Amer Sports One, Tyco, djuice dragons, Team News Corp* and *illbruck*. The VOR boats had completely dominated the battle for line honours in the Hobart race, but for the maxi *Nicorette*, which finished 15 minutes astern of *ASSA ABLOY* and was the second yacht to arrive. Both *Tyco* and *Amer Sports Too* were later declared nonfinishers in the Hobart race, *Tyco* because it did not comply with a radio safety report requirement when entering Bass Strait and *Amer Sports Too* because they received outside assistance off Tasmania's east coast (a replacement forestay fitting was delivered to them by boat). Neither incident would affect their overall result on Leg Three of the VOR — they weren't deemed to have breached any VOR rules, which applied for the entire stage.

With the six yachts sailing into Hobart so closely together, the scene was set for a great start to the second part of this leg, the 1400 miles across the Tasman Sea to Auckland. Each yacht would restart at the entrance to the Derwent River just 210 minutes after arriving in Hobart.

The pit stop at the dock created a charged atmosphere. Each yacht tied up so the skippers could do media interviews and Jez grabbed the opportunity to officially present their $10 000 prize to the bushfire appeal. The crews grabbed handfuls of fresh food and carried out quick maintenance checks. They looked longingly as Hobart race sailors stepped ashore and headed for the Customs House Hotel to begin their traditional post-race celebrations. For the Volvo race crews those celebrations were days away in Auckland.

Amer Sports Too arrived at the entrance to the Derwent as the others were leaving. It was an exceptional effort just to be there but, sadly, the crew would be delayed in Hobart an additional 24 hours while their rudder was repaired.

For the leading pack it was still anyone's leg. The only certainty was that it was going to be physically and mentally draining — because of the pressures associated with the Hobart race, which each crew had treated as a sprint.

Ross:

> *Day 4 — Things have been a little stressful with the finish in Hobart and the restart. Doing the two legs — Sydney to Hobart and Hobart to Auckland — is very similar to running a 10 000-metre race and then being asked to run a marathon. The Hobart race didn't finish the way we wanted. We sailed a fantastic leg but then got stuffed in Storm Bay, with everyone sailing around us while we sat in a hole with no wind. At least* illbruck *was with us. Everyone started again in Hobart within 40 minutes of each other and right now the fleet is within five miles. ASSA ABLOY has made a big move north while the rest of us are sticking together. The next 24 hours are going to be very interesting.*

The crew is really tired after the Hobart race and, as you can imagine, a little stressed. They are grateful that the normal watch system is up and running, in which they get three hours' sleep (in a sleeping bag) in one go, instead of the one hour (in their wet-weather gear) during the Hobart race. They are also, to my surprise, enjoying the freeze-dried food, but I think it may be because they had to eat three-day-old bread rolls during the Hobart leg. I'd like to add that I didn't have anything to do with the food ...

That move by *ASSA ABLOY* — a dogleg change of course that took them just 12 miles to the north of their original track — was the telling factor for this leg. After arriving in Auckland skipper Neal McDonald revealed that the move was based on information provided before the start by their race meteorologist, who was confident there was more favourable wind in the north. Incredibly, despite all other teams being able to source similar weather information, the *ASSA ABLOY* team was the only one to come up with this analysis of the developing weather pattern, i.e. to make a move to the north in search of a better breeze. Once that breeze was found, they were told they should change course towards the northern tip of New Zealand and sail near parallel to their opponents. Seeing the move *ASSA ABLOY* made, Grant Dalton, aboard *Amer Sports One*, decided there was little to lose, so he opted to split the difference between the yachts in the south and *ASSA ABLOY*'s chosen course. This tactical move was well rewarded, as *Amer Sports One* consolidated on the second place they held going into Hobart.

The others could only watch and hope that somewhere along the track the two bolters would be trapped by a calm spot, presenting the opportunity for a catch-up. Ross Field took time out to explain the frustration associated with watching *ASSA ABLOY* and *Amer Sports One* sail away after making their ever-so-slight course deviation to the north: 'We have 6.5 knots of wind from a direction of 206 degrees, and the forecast says we should have 6.5 knots from 240 degrees. The forecast also says that *ASSA ABLOY* should have no wind, but she has — not a lot, but from a direction that is sending her on a better course to Cape Reinga [the northern cape of New Zealand]. Peter Isler and I have been in the nav. station scratching our heads for most of the day. We've done well on *illbruck* and the others who are south of us, but not well on the boats in the north. This is all very confusing because everything says that *ASSA* and *Amer One* just shouldn't be going as well as they are. There is a bonus though — a beautiful night: full moon, cool on deck, quiet and smooth seas. The only noise is the odd click of a winch, the flap of a sail and a loud snore from Barney Walker. It's a vast contrast to the bash and crash we've had over the past few days.'

With outright points leader *illbruck* remaining on the southerly track and *Tyco* close at hand, Ross would explain later that *Team News Corp* had little option but to cover the race favourite: 'We didn't want to let *illbruck* go. Peter and I didn't think it was wise to break away from the pack and set our own course for Cape Reinga when we were still 500 miles out. Besides that, we figured we were in good company — the three of us [*Team News Corp*, *Tyco* and *illbruck*] couldn't all be wrong. In hindsight, of course, going north was the right thing to do, but the guys who are lower in the points table can afford to take risks, whereas the other guys can't. We had an invaluable opportunity to line up on this leg against *illbruck* and, for that matter, *Tyco*, and really test ourselves over a considerable distance against a known quantity.'

The year 2001 didn't end on a high note for *Team News Corp*, *illbruck*, *Tyco* or *djuice*. *ASSA ABLOY* and *Amer Sports One* found an open gate and bolted. That small course change translated into stronger wind and in 24 hours *ASSA* was 85 miles ahead and *Amer* 62! First and second place on this leg were as good as decided.

The trio, *Team News Corp*, *illbruck* and *Tyco*, were destined to finish third, fourth and fifth, but the order was far from certain.

Every point earned might well be critical to the end result on this nine-leg stoush, so the pressure was exceptional. To lose half a mile between position reports was a morale-sapping experience. To gain was a massive confidence boost. But it was just as important to know when to come off the pace as it was to put the foot down.

Ross Halcrow — trimmer, *illbruck*:

Day 5 — We changed to an asymmetric spinnaker, the conditions were nice, 25 knots of wind, and we were on course. There was a line of black clouds approaching us from behind; we were prepared for the wind to build as the clouds were getting closer. What we weren't prepared for was the cloud line to be a southerly buster ... the wind went from 25 knots to 35 knots ... we put the bow down and accelerated into a left turn. This was what I would call the biggest wipeout I have ever been a part of. We lay the boat over. The movement was so violent ... I was trimming the sail at the time; I was thrown off the sail stack and went into a front flip towards the leeward side of the boat (and the ocean). On my way down I hit the mainsheet winch with the backside of my hip bone (fully swollen now, and I am now hobbling around the boat). I managed to grab hold of one of the leeward rope tail bags on my way past, to stop myself from continuing on to go through the life lines [safety rails]; Tony also got a hold of my ankle as I went past him. All in all it was a little too close for comfort — the last thing I wanted was a swim.

Had Halcrow finished up in the ocean he could have been in for some more surprises — of a natural kind, lurking just below the surface.

Stig Westergaard — trimmer/helmsman, *djuice dragons*:

I had a close encounter with tons of flesh yesterday. I was at the helm, steering in my usual 'tunnel' of concentration, when suddenly, just three metres in front of the boat a massive whale appeared, probably two to three times the size of the boat, or so it appeared. I must have had 200 strokes in heartbeat instantly (my usual max is 185) and had to change course quite a bit not to

hit it. But, boy, was it a great experience ... Definitely one
of the things I had looked forward to ... just to be close to
one of these gracious creatures.

With so much happening there was little time to realise it was New Year's Eve in the middle of the Tasman Sea. In fact, it was a miserable introduction to 2002, with the fleet reaching across a breeze that blew at up to 30 knots — the wettest and least pleasant angle on these boats.

Jez:

... Right now [New Year's Day] we are locked in a tight
battle for third with illbruck and Tyco, 250 miles from
the top of New Zealand, reaching along in 16 knots of
air with a bit of sunshine. There's a small chance of
drying out after a couple of days of hard reaching. This
leg seems to have been the hardest physically so far. I
don't know if it is because of the stopover in Hobart and
the fact that we haven't recovered from the trip down
there properly, but moving the ton of wet sails around
the boat is a daunting task at the moment. We've had a
lot of gear changes in the last few days, requiring us to
change sails and move all the gear around in the boat,
which has been draining on the body's reserves. This has
been accompanied by a continual soaking, so that the
boat below smells like it is inhabited by 12 wet
labradors.

Just over two days to go, with the leading two boats
looking hard to catch, unless there is a big hole waiting for
them (it has happened before). Yacht racing is definitely
not over until the fat lady sings. We are ready for any
windows of opportunity that might open up for us.

There was growing consensus among the race's most experienced ocean sailors that seasickness was more prevalent than ever before, possibly because of the more violent motion experienced on this latest crop of high-performance yachts.

When conditions are this unpleasant, seasickness can descend on a crew. *Amer Sports Too*'s Emma Westmacott felt that it seemed to be catching more and more of the sailors during the race.

Emma Westmacott — watch leader, *Amer Sports Too*

I don't know if it is something to do with the boats becoming more aggressive, but a lot of people who don't normally have a problem are coming down with it. I haven't been seasick for years, but in the first leg I had it badly in the Bay of Biscay. It's a feeling that makes you want to jump off the side of the boat and end it all. It's miserable, you don't feel like doing anything, you get lethargic and you get tired. You lose interest in anything except in how manky you feel, and pretty much each time you move, or change your environment, you throw up ... You just think, 'How am I going to get down those steps, take my foul weather gear off, be thrown around, hang it up and get into my bunk without being sick?' And then once you have taken your foulies off, it is all over, because you can't come up on deck to be sick because you would get soaking wet. People get wet and then they get cold ... It is something you have to combat early, or accept the fact that you have a problem with it. Once you're actually sick, you only get better when the breeze subsides.

Chris Nicholson, a trimmer/helmsman on *Amer Sports One*, describes the debilitating effects of seasickness as being like your worst hangover, plus it affects the whole body, not just your mind or your stomach: 'When you're that sick, you're trying so hard not to move around anywhere, you have no energy and no control over where you're moving, so you just keep the body as still as possible. These boats are undermanned and you still have to sail. The guys would probably let you stay in your bunk, but you can't, you just have to get on and do your job. There's no eating because that just comes straight back up. You still have to try to keep some fluids down … But even that tends to come up as well …'

Ross:

> Day 8 — Wind of 24 knots from 322 degrees. Boat speed 16 knots and very, very wet.
>
> The battle continues. What fantastic racing. When we started in Hobart three days ago illbruck was 0.5 miles behind. She passed us once, we got her back and now the two of us have been locked together ever since, no more than a 1-mile separation.
>
> We're gaining so much information about our boat, sails and trim — perfect two boat testing, but also testing on the nerves as we monitor the radar every 10 minutes.
>
> It's amazing how the crew responds to having another boat so close all the time. There's a new sense of urgency as they push themselves, even though they are dog-tired after the Sydney to Hobart race. We are extremely fortunate to have a fantastic crew.

ASSA ABLOY held a 21-mile lead over Amer Sports One. The real fight was another 26 miles back, the battle for third place … and it wasn't going to be easy. Sailing under skies as grey and heavy as lead after one of the most intense battles so far, Team News Corp came into the City of Sails in fifth place, just 6 minutes, 15 seconds out of third place. The toughest leg had dealt the harshest blow.

Gordon Maguire:

> This was the first time we experienced some genuine bad luck. Yachting is one of those games that relies on an element of luck when it comes to the weather patterns that you cannot predict. As a result it's also about ups and downs, and it's very much about controlling those downs.

We very nearly finished third. The only thing we could do was apply a feel-good attitude to the result; we had to say to ourselves, 'We only got a fifth, but it was so close to a third.' Sometimes you don't necessarily need the result on paper to make a team feel good. A team feels good about how it performs, not about how it is perceived outside the team. And that was an important leg ... to know that we could take illbruck on, boat to boat, and show that we should have beaten them. The big plus was we then knew that later on, if ever we should go bow to bow with them again, we will beat them.

Team News Corp's downfall came when the westerly breeze the crew were expecting on the approach to Auckland never appeared. Due to their total points tally in the race to date it was more important for *Team News Corp* to try to beat *illbruck* rather than *Tyco*. As far as they were concerned the *Tyco* crew could sail their own race to the finish line.

During the whole leg from Hobart to Auckland, *Team News Corp* and *illbruck* were never more than 4 miles apart. Coming into Auckland Harbour *News Corp* passed *illbruck*, which then altered course slightly and benefited from a change in wind direction. This was enough to see *illbruck* regain the lead by just metres, keep *Team News Corp* covered all the way to the finish line and claim fourth behind *Tyco*. A despondent Ross Field had never seen racing so close, but he still believed *Team News Corp* could win the event. He was more than happy with the boat development program, the yacht's speed and the crew work against *illbruck*, which was the yardstick.

Jez:

[Hobart to Auckland] was the hardest leg so far ... very, very hard. You look around the fleet and talk to the people and everyone is physically drained. I suspect the problems came from treating the Hobart race as a sprint, then having the stopover. It was basically two races, not

one leg. By about the third day — after leaving Hobart — we were absolutely exhausted . . . running on empty.

What this leg did do is show the others that we are fast, that we sail the boat well and that we are smart. Sadly, though, yacht racing is a cruel beast to play with. You can get into the lead, only to see it smashed away. Yes, we are disappointed in the result on this leg, but not the performance. We sailed the boat as well as anyone out there.

Virtually the minute *Team News Corp* arrived at the dock in Auckland the sun broke through heavy grey clouds and shone like a brilliant spotlight on the yacht.

Was it an omen for the next leg?

Top *ASSA ABLOY* sails up the Derwent River to claim line honours in the Sydney to Hobart yacht race.

Centre You're welcome. *ASSA ABLOY*'s skipper, Neal McDonald, rubs noses as part of a traditional Maori welcome in Auckland.

Bottom The VO 60s are rigged and ready to leave Auckland's Viaduct Basin for the start of Leg Four.

All images *Rick Tomlinson*

≫ AUCKLAND
TO RIO DE JANEIRO

We would have lasted only half an hour in survival suits.

God knows what might have happened.

It's just lucky that we are all alive.

GURRA KRANTZ — SKIPPER, *TEAM SEB*

uckland was like a homecoming for *Team News Corp*. The syndicate had been based there for training while the race boat was being built, and with a strong Kiwi contingent in the team, it was very comfortable having so many family and friends around after three arduous legs of the race. And for those who were non-New Zealanders the legendary Kiwi hospitality made it feel almost like being at home.

But being home with his partner and young family proved to be too great an emotional burden for watch leader Jeff Scott. The highly valued helmsman told Ross and Jez that he would be leaving the team once they reached Rio de Janeiro to return to his family and reality — and his other love, fishing. He missed home too much.

There was one permanent change to the crew in Auckland: Gundy off, Nigel King on. It was a move Ross, Jez and other key crewmembers made to bring more strength to the team sailing at the forward end of the cockpit.

And there was one permanent more major announcement. Ross and Jez decided it was time to declare officially that they were co-skippers for the campaign, a secret they had held since Cape Town. They felt the timing was right to inform the media, in particular, of what everyone inside the campaign already knew.

THE SAYING GOES that any New Zealander who doesn't own a boat knows someone who does. The country boasts the highest per capita rate of boat ownership in the world.

This tiny nation's enthusiasm for sailing and the Volvo Ocean Race was blatantly apparent on the morning of 27 January 2002 when around 45 000 people crammed every vantage point around Auckland's Viaduct Basin to bid farewell to the fleet on what could be the most treacherous leg of the race — a 6700-mile stretch to Rio de Janeiro, Brazil. This leg would require the yachts to sail deeper into the brutal Southern Ocean than they had on the second leg, and round the world's most treacherous neck of land, Cape Horn, then sail into the steamy tropics of South America to reach the finish.

The enthusiastic farewell at the Basin spilled onto the water, where the largest spectator fleet seen so far for the commencement of any leg of the race was waiting for the start. In the cavalcade that followed the firing of the start gun, it was *Tyco*, skippered by Kiwi Kevin Shoebridge, that led the charge out to the more distant of the two turning marks. *Team News Corp* was part of the leading pack, just 85 seconds off the pace. At that final mark the yachts started to nose into a gentle ocean swell. All crews began preparing to turn towards the Southern Ocean and Cape Horn, one of the most isolated points on the planet.

Soon after passing the mark the *Team News Corp* crew made their first tactical move. Scanning the horizon, Steve Cotton's eyes locked onto what he, as a resident of Auckland, knew to be an approaching sea breeze. The decision onboard was to keep sailing offshore towards the wind, while the rest of the fleet tacked and sailed south. It wasn't long before Cotton's calculated gamble began to deliver the goods. They found more breeze from a favourable direction, tacked, and sailed into the lead. From there it was going to be a drag race south to the strong westerly winds that would propel them at high velocity towards Cape Horn.

AFTER FIVE DAYS of racing out of Auckland, this leg to Rio was notable for two things. The Roaring Forties were barely whispering and the racing was incredibly close. The wind had been so light that the yachts had not seen a splash of water come over the bow and onto the deck. And the first seven yachts were still within sight of each other.

It was, however, a scene that would change within 24 hours. A cold front was charging in from the southwest, straight off the ice of Antarctica.

The only drama on that initial stretch was a self-inflicted wound for *Team SEB*'s skipper, Gurra Krantz. During a tack, when moving all the gear, he accidentally injured himself on a knife sticking out of a tool bag. It looked a bit messy for a while, but after treatment by sail trimmer 'Doctor' Glen Kessels he was fine. The cut on his wrist was glued together with superglue!

Alby:

Day 5 — Life aboard Team News Corp *is good and conditions are excellent. This restart has been a dream run. But down below, life has picked up where we left off and everyone is back into their little routines. Justin continues to leave his clothing strewn around the boat from bow to stern; Shreda has little bits of power bars or minute packs of nuts stashed into every nook and Barney (aka 'The Barn') has taken up his normal, prized bunk in the stern. This bunk, because of its position at the very back, is the darkest and quietest and allows for the best sleeping. At the start of every leg someone will say that they are having that bunk, but when the time comes it is The Barn who is racked out in the palace.*

The cold front arrived and *Team News Corp* was driven further south than any of its rivals. Suddenly there was an element of shock among the crew. They didn't like what they were seeing and Ross's words before leaving Auckland were echoing in their ears: 'You're not going to see any ice on this leg … we're not going to see anything. On *Yamaha* we saw one iceberg, but we went down to 63 degrees south.' But when they set out from Auckland neither Ross nor anyone else knew that this time around the ice would be 800 miles north of the usual limit for that time of year.

Ross:

Day 7 — Never seen so many icebergs and growlers in all my sailing in the Southern Ocean. Spotted our first iceberg, then all of a sudden sighted many others with growlers everywhere. We were sailing through small bits of ice at 23 knots and at one stage we passed within 20 feet of a growler. Global warming? I say yes — there is ice breaking off the ice cap all the time and I have never seen ice on this part of the race before. I am seriously worried now with night approaching. We have the radar on full-

time and are praying like hell we miss. Jokes that the icebergs go away at night have disappeared and there is real concern.

Regardless of the danger, *Team News Corp* continued to drive hard on a course that took them to near 60 degrees south. The next day they were in the lead ...

Ross:

Day 8 — Sailing in 23 knots from the southwest, spinnaker and full main. We are making a good 17 knots. Very pleasant sailing, but it's cold, very cold. Had snow earlier on this morning and have only sighted one iceberg, which is very encouraging but it will still be the full radar watch tonight. Life onboard is the same old eat, sleep and sail. Just got up for the next watch (had been dreaming about a warm, dry bed — instead of a cold, damp sleeping bag) and am waiting on lunch — nasi goreng with rice — nothing like you get at home, but it will fill the gap.

Cape Horn is seven days away and then we'll be heading north. The cold down here slowly gets to you ...

Nick:

Day 8 — Icebergs are very scary things ... and I have a faint suspicion that they don't go to sleep at night as some people have theorised. Maybe I'm getting older and learning just how precarious our existence is. All I know is that they worry me a lot more than they did eight years ago. Maybe the fascination of seeing an iceberg has worn off. We know that it is better to pass them to leeward as 'bergs drift faster with the wind than the broken-off growlers, which are much harder to see.

...Everything is damp on board and the boat seems to continually develop new places to let the water in. The

slosh of ice-cold water in the leeward bilge beside my nav. station is not a very warming sound. So it is surprising how cheerful everyone is and how good the team spirit is. We haven't made the most of our lead, but we still have it, so things could be worse.

Conditions remained cold, bleak and generally miserable. The wind was gusting over 30 knots and the seas were building into ugly, angry mountains that reflected the threatening nature of the dark-grey sky. The yachts were thundering down wave after wave at breakneck speed under full spinnaker, with spray flying and bow waves exploding like massive avalanches.

For some crewmembers it wasn't all that bad. It was still snowing, and when you have never seen snow fall before it's a novelty ... at least for a brief time.

Anthony Nossiter — trimmer/helmsman, *djuice dragons*:

Day 9 — I didn't expect or hope to have to come to the Southern Ocean to see my first snowfall. It wasn't really a childhood dream to be sailing in the snow, but that is exactly what we've been doing for the day. The snow began at 6am; it's now 4pm and still falling. Billy Merrington [trimmer/helmsman] got me in the face with a snowball as a wake-up call this morning. At the time we were very excited to see snow (we're both Australian and don't see it much) but as the day has gone on our pleasure of sailing in snow is rapidly deteriorating. We are looking forward to sweating again after we round Cape Horn in about seven very long days and nights.

The crews were under relentless pressure, pushing things to the limit under as much sail as they dared carry. Racing was one thing — missing icebergs and growlers was another. Russian roulette seemed to be a safer pastime. The *Team News Corp* crew were doing an excellent job, weaving their way through a minefield of 'bergs and growlers day and night. They were in the Screaming Fifties. The radar was on around the clock as they probed the murky conditions for the 'berg or growler that could bring their race unstuck ... and threaten their lives.

By now the wind was so unpredictable that it was anyone's guess as to who would make the bigger gains. Conditions began to favour the yachts to the north. Being in the south, *Team News Corp* was one that lost out, slipping back to fourth place. The most significant gain went to *illbruck*, which burst forward from the middle of the pack. Finding the reaching conditions that suited his boat, skipper John Kostecki soon saw his charge holding a 26-mile lead over *Tyco*, with *Amer Sports One* and *News Corp* in close pursuit. More than 40 miles back were *djuice*, *ASSA ABLOY* and *Team SEB* with *Amer Sports Too* trailing the leader by 246 miles.

American Paul Cayard, who won the previous Volvo race as skipper of *EF Language*, had joined *Amer Sports One* for this leg, knowing only too well what the Southern Ocean had on offer. He reported back to race headquarters that their iceberg and growler count was growing by 10 per hour. At one stage, while watching the radar and seeing nothing, they sailed just 100 feet away from a growler that was 10 feet out of the water. It was a scary realisation of the dangers they faced when sailing at such high speed. Paul also told of the impact the cold was having on his ability to steer, and of an 80-foot wave that had to be seen to be believed: '... severe tendonitis. My grip strength in my left hand is 25 per cent of what it is normally, but my right hand is good — I'm still able to weave in and out of the 30-foot seas easily while we sit on 25 to 28 knots. My top speed was 32 knots. At one point, two or three waves came together to make one huge wave. We got up on top of it and looked down a 120-foot runway that was sloping at about 30 degrees. Everyone's eyes were huge; a phenomenal wave that Grant Dalton said was the biggest he had ever ridden.'

Jez:

> Day 9 — Snow and ice ... 58 south in the Southern
> Ocean, water temperature 2.8 degrees C, the ice is large
> 'bergs and there is no chance to build a snowman. The
> heater is running on overtime, gear bags are empty of

clothes and the extremities are numbing. Cape Horn is 2300 miles away with some heavy air forecast for the next few days. The racing is as tight as ever. Get ready for a wet ride.

Life below deck in this weather continued to be absolutely miserable. Everything was wet because it was so salty and the humidity was up to 100 per cent. The sails were all soaking wet; as were the crew's sleeping bags.

An interior heater helped warm up their socks and boots, but nothing was ever really dry — it was just a different shade of wetness.

Gordon Maguire describes the 'tolerable wet', and the 'intolerable wet': 'Tolerable wet is when you are warm, and intolerable wet is when you are cold, but in reality it's all the same wet. When you get into your wet sleeping bag it's sopping wet and cold. When you wake up four hours later it appears to be dry, but all you've done is warm up the wetness with your body heat. When you get out of the sleeping bag and put on your on-deck gear, the gear seems to be dry, but now you know it's wet because it's cold, and you're warm ...

'You work very hard to manage your extremities: your hands, face and feet; it's absolutely vital that you go on deck with your circulation alive in your hands and feet. If you go on a watch without getting the circulation back ... then you start to run the risk of serious circulation problems.'

Ross:

Day 9 — Conditions are bloody freezing. The heater is running six hours a day, and we had snow on deck. We're back in full Southern Ocean kit, which means it's taking us 30 minutes to get dressed, ready to face the outdoors. Icebergs are still a definite worry. I saw the biggest iceberg of my career yesterday. It was five miles wide, and five miles long.

Team News Corp's other Irishman, the dry-humoured Justin Slattery, was getting everything he'd bargained for on his inaugural race around the world. He had always dreamt of racing through the Southern Ocean, and he thought he'd seen everything on Leg Two, between Cape Town and Sydney: 'We had 10 days on that leg where we were absolutely hauling ... We were driving the yacht as hard as you could capably drive a yacht. It was an incredible feeling, watch after watch, day after day, having the boat planing, doing 20-plus knots and breaking the 24-hour record. On Leg Four the speed was similar but "ice world" brought disaster considerably closer. It wasn't a case of if, but when we would hit ice. If you said you weren't frightened you were either a liar or mentally unstable ... Unlike heavy air downwind sailing, which can be wild but controllable, in these conditions control is totally out of your hands. Knowing you cannot control what might happen is not a good feeling. All the time you think about what you're going to do ... You know where every piece of safety kit is on the boat but, incredibly, you don't think about dying. I always hold a very strong feeling that if things go wrong we will still manage to get out of there.'

Staring at intense danger was a haunting experience for the helmsmen on each watch. No one explains the experience more vividly than *Team News Corp*'s Gordon Maguire: 'The evening watch is always the worst because it gets dark at the end of the watch, and in the darkness everything becomes bigger, and noisier, and windier, and scarier. It's only a four-hour watch, but it seems longer. At the end, when the last light is setting in, you look at your watch and say to yourself, "Only 20 minutes to go. OK, we're only in 30 knots of wind; the boat's doing 25 knots; we've got the Code 6 spinnaker up, full mainsail, we're under control." It's kind of another day at the office. You want it to be over. It's your turn to go down below.

'Your feet are like iceblocks; you haven't felt them in three hours. Your hands are completely numb. You have the wheel in your hand, you know it's there, but you don't really have the feel of it. Your face and nose, particularly around your nostrils, is red-raw from the salt spray and your eyes feel as though they're bleeding. It feels like they're bleeding from the inside but you know they're not — it's just from the salt spray constantly in your face. You look at your watch again and you think, "Eighteen minutes to go; it's going to be alright; it's going to be alright."

'The atmosphere is dank … foggy and misty with a hundred per cent humidity. Visibility is about 400 yards, so you are actually just running with the radar on the whole time. The next moment the navigator sticks his head up and says, "Iceberg on the bow, one mile!" You do a quick mental calculation — that's two or three minutes, closing speed!'

When sailing downwind at around 25 knots the helmsman has a 10-degree envelope in which to change course. If he steers up (towards the direction of the wind) more than 5 degrees they wipe out … broach, and if he steers down more than 5 degrees the yacht will gybe, breaking the mast. The call 'iceberg on the bow!' means he has two or three minutes to get the boat around it. Hearts are racing and everyone on deck starts getting twitchy. They're all thinking the same thing: is it a big 'berg or a small 'berg? Should the course change be to the left or the right? During one of these tense moments Gordon Maguire was at the helm. He asked the obvious question of navigator Steve Cotton: 'Which side, up or down?' Steve disappeared below deck, shouting, 'Wait a moment!' Gordon had to curb his impatience, knowing that while there were only two minutes until a possible impact Steve had to check the actual location of the iceberg on the radar. Steve reappeared: 'It's on the port bow … come up a little bit.' The crew filled up the water ballast tanks for more stability and the course was changed 5 degrees to starboard. There was a collective sigh of relief — they knew where the 'berg was; everything was under control.

Then Steve slipped down below again, back to watch the radar. The crew counted down the time and peered through the murk, trying to find the 'berg. Gordon looked at his watch, just waiting to finish his time on deck. Then Steve reappeared in the companionway, shouting, 'Second iceberg on the starboard bow, half a mile!'

Gordon yelled, 'You're kidding me, is this the same iceberg? Are they joined? This could be one iceberg with two peaks.' His thoughts flashed back to school: *Shit, was it 80 per cent below the water, or 20 per cent? It's 80 per cent.* He called out to Steve, 'What's the gap between them?' By then the 'berg was so close they'd run out of options. They had a 'berg to the left and a 'berg to the right. There was only one thing they could do: go through the middle.

At that moment one of the younger crewmembers turned round, looked at Gordon and said, 'What if they're connected?'

Gordon looked back at him and replied, 'Then we're going to die.' He wasn't joking. They charged on through between what turned out to be two 'bergs.

The water between the 'bergs was strewn with bits of ice, from the size of a bus to the size of a beach ball. If they hit something bigger than two or three metres across it would send them down — the hull would be compromised and they would sink in a few minutes.

They were still doing 25 knots. Alby stood behind Gordon, calling the gaps between the bigger bits of ice. They were dodging left and right, going to the limit of their 10-degree safety zone at times. Alby was calling out, 'Go up 2 degrees; go up 2; down 5; up 10 ... oh my God, up 5!' Gordon pleaded with him to leave out the expletives — 'oh my God' was a waste of precious seconds.

They hit a lot of small pieces, then popped out the other side between the two 'bergs, and a minute later it was all over. Steve came back on deck to give the all-clear and there was another collective sigh. Gordon felt the sweat running down his back and starting to freeze, and suddenly realised that he was actually colder and more miserable than he had been in his entire life. He thought about his kids, and all the things that would have changed if he didn't actually make it through that gap.

It was time for Gordon's watch to go below and the new watch, led by Jeff Scott, to come up on deck. Scotty asked Gordon how things had been going. 'Don't ask. Just don't ask,' was his reply. He reported on the sailing conditions, how strong the wind had been and how the boat was set up, then went down below, took his gloves off and saw that his hands were shaking.

'I went to my kit bag looking for some dry clothes to get into, and in my wallet was a picture of my family; my wife and two young daughters. I looked at it and thought, "I don't need to do this any more. I'm 40 years old and I have got a beautiful family. Time to move on. I'm over it."'

He climbed into his bunk, snuggled up and tried not to be there. 'I took my mind elsewhere. I ... was with my wife and kids. I was in total denial because in your bunk you are helpless. The other watch is now in control. It's your life in their hands. While you're on deck their life is in your hands. To me that's one of the biggest pressures. The anxiety of it all. When you're driving a yacht in these conditions the average guy on the street has no idea of the stress involved when you have someone's life in your hands. It destroys you emotionally. I just lay there in my bunk, unable to sleep because it takes about an hour for your heart to slow down. I lay there thinking, then I heard the navigator saying, "Iceberg on the bow, three miles," and then, "Holy shit, this is a big one. It's a kilometre long, right on the bow." I just zipped up my sleeping bag and went deeper into denial. I was snuggled up in bed at home with my wife, all the time thinking, "I'm not here any more."'

WITH EVERY ONE of the 97 sailors in the race living on the edge of a precipice of potential disaster it seemed inevitable that one of the yachts would go over the brink sooner rather than later.

Team News Corp would be the one ...

Ross:

> *Day 10 — We hit a small 'berg while doing 21 knots! I was steering and all I felt was a loud crash on the hull and then the rudder. The guys below rushed into the bow and checked the interior, but we appeared to be OK.*
>
> *I am bloody worried. This is dangerous ... there are icebergs everywhere. There are growlers floating nowhere near the 'bergs. We thought we were clear of the ice when we hit this 'berg.*
>
> *It's now night-time and the off-watch is huddled in the nav. station looking at the radar. We've had a shocking day: broken sails, battens, and halyards. The boat's a shambles, sails everywhere downstairs and the guys are sleeping in their survival suits. We're sleeping*

*with our feet forward — that's because if we hit
something you don't damage yourself too much.*

This is sport in the extreme.

For some time before hitting the ice, Ross, Nick and Steve had talked about taking a new course to the northeast, where they expected stronger winds and faster sailing over the next few days. The collision with the iceberg made the decision for them — they were heading to safer waters. The only problem was that, to sail the optimum course, they needed to use their fractional spinnaker — but the halyard for that sail had broken hours earlier and it was too dangerous to send someone aloft to replace it.

'If we hadn't broken our fractional halyard we would have probably been in the lead at Cape Horn,' Ross declared later, 'because we would've been able to sail better angles to get north and towards the Cape. Since we could only use the headsail we had to sail slightly higher and, therefore, a greater distance while we fixed the fractional halyard.'

Still, *Team News Corp* made significant inroads into *illbruck*'s lead. In one 24-hour period, soon after changing course, they covered 30 miles more than any other yacht.

At this stage the fleet was at the most remote point on the planet from civilisation. But they didn't have time to think about their isolation until Day 12, the day *Team SEB* was dismasted with near-fatal consequences!

There were icebergs everywhere. It was pitch-black, the middle of the night, and a snowstorm howled around them. The wind leapt from 32 to 48 knots which, with the high density of the air in the region, is the equivalent of 60 to 65 knots in normal conditions.

The sea condition was severe; the waves were mountainous and unpredictable. *Team SEB* had already been submerged several times, jumping from one wave straight into the back of the wave ahead, then going straight through it.

Gurra Krantz — skipper, *Team SEB*:
*We were heading north at the time and starting to get out
of that maniac land. As a skipper you have a knot in your*

*stomach all the time; every second you feel uncomfortable
... at least I do, being responsible for so many lives.*

*People ask about slowing down in those conditions,
but if you slow down to be safe you have to go from 25 to
5 knots. Slowing down from 25 to 20 knots doesn't make
any difference. But if you slow down to 5 knots, then you
may as well go north and go home. Alternatively, you
keep on putting a gun to your head and keep the pedal on
the metal.*

*I was below, and we were scanning for squalls on the
radar. We saw this big squall coming and knew there was
no way out of it ... We just hoped that it was no worse
than the previous squalls we'd had. We could handle
them. After it's all over you say, 'Jesus Christ that was
scary,' but you still have a feeling that you can take on
another one.*

*But when this one hit us, the sensation in my body
was almost like resignation: 'This is it. This is not going to
work.' All of a sudden this big hammer came along that
was determined to get us.*

Tom Braidwood, who runs the foredeck on *Team SEB*, saw the black
cloud looming. The squall hit them hard and kept rising: 32, 33, 34, 35, 36
knots ... 38, 39, 40. He unclipped his harness and moved towards the martin
breaker, a device rigged to release the spinnaker or gennaker immediately in
a dangerous situation, located in the cockpit and, as the wind speed reached
41, 42, they started to roll.

Scott Beavis — bowman, *Team SEB*:

*The mainsail and gennaker were trimmed on and we
started rolling back to windward. I moved across and
started grinding the mainsail in. The third roll to leeward
was a biggy. I was still grinding the main as the boat
rolled to windward. This time it didn't feel so good. Tony,*

Top left Still managing to smile, the *Amer Sports Too* crew head for Halifax, Nova Scotia, under jury rig after the yacht was dismasted on Leg Seven. They have the trysail set along with an upside-down storm jib. *Klaartje Zulderbaan*

Top right The *illbruck* crew pushed the yacht in an Atlantic storm and achieved a world 24-hour record run of 484 nautical miles. *Ray Davies*

Centre Winning means grinning, as is obvious with the *illbruck* crew after they were first to finish on the leg from Annapolis to La Rochelle. *Rick Tomlinson*

Bottom Ready to race. The fleet is lined up on the evening before the start of Leg Eight from La Rochelle. *Rick Tomlinson*

Top Not buoyed with success. *ASSA ABLOY* tows the starting buoy after it fouled on its keel at the start of Leg Eight. *Jon Nash/djuice dragons*

Centre A taste of things to come for the girls aboard *Amer Sports Too* as they set out on the rugged first stage of the leg from La Rochelle to Gothenburg. *Rick Tomlinson*

Bottom *illbruck* is almost obscured by a breaking wave soon after setting sail from La Rochelle. *Rick Tomlinson*

Top left After a rough start it was a smooth sailing into Gothenburg. *Team News Corp* ghosts towards the welcoming lights of the Swedish city.

Top right Matt Humphries holds aloft the crystal trophy awarded to the *Team News Corp* crew for their third place into Gothenburg.

Centre left Barracking for his home side. Jez cheers for England during a World Cup soccer match televised in Gothenburg.

Centre right Intense concentration is obvious as the crew follows Jez's race strategy on the eve of the crucial final leg to Kiel in Germany.

Bottom left Helping or helpless? Bart Simpson was roped in to help in Gothenburg.

Bottom right *Team News Corp* supporters crowd the dock in Gothenburg to farewell the crew for the start of the final leg and a possible third place overall.

All images *Richard Langdon/Ocean Images*

Top The start of the final leg from Gothenburg to Kiel was the most spectacular of the entire race. Well over 100 000 spectators took up every available vantage point on shore.

Bottom The fleet had to sail through myriad small islands outside Gothenburg. *From left to right*: *ASSA ABLOY*, *Team News Corp*, *djuice dragons* and *SEB*.

Right There were enthusiastic yet chaotic scenes on the water as a massive spectator fleet farewelled the yachts from Gothenburg. Almost anything that floated was out on the water.

All images *Richard Langdon/Ocean Images*

Top Gothenburg turned on a gloriously sunny day for the start. More than 2000 craft of all shapes and sizes lined the course to see the VOR fleet leave.

Bottom Stablemates *Amer Sports One* and *Amer Sports Too* pass under Denmark's Osterrenden Bridge in a near calm. Each yacht had a crewmember hoisted up the mast to search for signs of wind on the water surface.

All images *Rick Tomlinson*

Top There was a hero's welcome home for John Kostecki's *illbruck* team as they sailed the German yacht into Kiel and claimed outright victory in the VOR.

Bottom As the wind decreased the frustration increased, for *Team News Corp* on its final approach to Kiel. It was like racing on a pond.

Top left Despite the late hour and the disappointment associated with the final result, the *Team News Corp* crew were heartened by the welcome in Kiel. Flares went up and more than 5000 people were on the dock to greet them.

Top right Emotionally shattered. Jez Fanstone shows the strain after arriving in Kiel.

Centre The smiles came back when the *Team News Corp* crew received their race medals at the official trophy presentation in Kiel.

Bottom left What racing around the planet is all about. *illbruck*'s John Kostecki holds aloft the VOR winner's Waterford Crystal trophy at the end of the final leg.

Bottom right The crews and their supporters celebrate the end of the VOR at the post-race party.

All images *Richard Langdon/Ocean Images*

the watch leader, yelled, 'Guys, it's gone ...' describing his control over the boat in a relatively calm manner. The last numbers he remembers seeing were boat speed 28 knots and wind speed 42 knots.

We rolled to windward and the cockpit filled with water. I was the only one of us clipped on at the time and managed to grab a rail. Tom wrapped himself around the leeward (now upper) grinding pedestal and was also underwater. Woos [Gareth Cook, helmsman/trimmer], who was next to the wheel, grabbed the primary winch shaft. Tony held on to the centre of the wheel. Woos remembered struggling for breath — that's how far under we were. With our [companionway] hatch now 1 metre underwater all the guys in the bunks below were woken (if not already) with a ton or so of icy water flooding the cabin.

Bang! The unmistakable sound of carbon blowing up. We rolled upright; the mast had twisted off about 2 metres above the boom from the force of the first [bottom] spreader hitting the water at 28 knots. We were lucky it broke, otherwise the boat would have filled with water and sunk.

'Where is everyone?' I thought. I knew they weren't clipped on. 'Sweet, everyone is here.'

The deck light ... illuminated the carnage: a sorry-looking stump, a broken boom, most of the windward sail stack in the water, and the bottom end of the mast hanging over the side. Work began on cutting the thing loose, we had it free within an hour and a half and were [jury rigged] and sailing in four hours.

Gurra describes how the mast literally twisted out of the boat when the spreaders hit the water: 'Because it broke, the boat slowly righted itself. If it hadn't broken we would have stayed on our side because, apart from the pressure of wind in the sails, we had 1700 kilograms of water ballast and about a tonne of wet sails holding her down ... the decks would have been awash in those seas. We would have lasted only half an hour in survival suits. God knows what might have happened. It's just lucky that we're all alive.'

WHILE *TEAM SEB* limped towards a port near the tip of Cape Horn, where it would be met by a ship and freighted to Rio, the remainder of the fleet began escaping the clutches of the horror world of icebergs.

Ross:

> *Finally saw the sun today. No more icebergs. Survival suits have been packed away and the crew are working on the damage. Our northerly route is paying off and we believe we'll have more pressure in the north for the entire trip to Cape Horn. I'm sure the other boats have had damage too. We are definitely not an 'if only' boat and the guys deal with these situations extremely well. It's been an excellent recovery and it's very nice to be gaining on each sked, instead of taking those massive losses ...*

For all the crews, knowing that their death-defying voyage through the ice was now behind them was like being given a pardon and free passage. *Team News Corp*'s Justin Slattery was adamant that the only ice he wanted to see in the future was in a gin and tonic.

On Day 15 came the ultimate achievement for any round-the-world sailor when the Cape was reached and rounded. Cape Horn is considered to be the most perilous of the world's capes. It has claimed the lives of more seamen than all the others and has presented unparalleled obstacles. In 1904, for example, horrendously unfavourable weather for months on end resulted in the four-masted sailing ship *Edward Sewell* taking 92 days to negotiate the passage from the Atlantic Ocean to the Pacific.

Team News Corp's blast away from the ice and to the northeast certainly worked. They'd made remarkable gains on the leaders, at one stage recovering 150 miles in 48 hours. While *illbruck* had maintained the advantage at Cape Horn it had established days earlier, four other yachts were having a sensational race for what was then the minor places. At the Cape, *illbruck*'s lead was 65 miles over *Amer Sports One*. The next three yachts and their distance from the leader were: *Tyco* 70 miles; *Team News Corp* 81; *ASSA ABLOY* 84. *djuice dragons* was 122 miles in arrears, while *Amer Sports Too* had dropped back to more than 560 miles off the pace. The wounded *Team SEB* was another 360 miles astern making very slow progress east. There were questions as to whether or not they'd even make it to Rio in time for the next start.

Ross:

> Day 15 — We're around [Cape Horn] and heading north to the warmth of the tropics. It's the first time I have seen the Horn on a bright sunny day. It's possibly the last time I will see it, but I've said that before. We were only 1 mile offshore. It was a fantastic sight — the raw rock that's been scarred by thousands of years of howling winds and raging seas. There are no trees to be seen, I guess it's too windy for them to grow.
>
> We're in good shape, in contact with the leaders — have ASSA ABLOY three miles back. It's amazing that yesterday we had 35 knots of wind and now 3 knots, but it's a welcome break. It's warmer and now it doesn't take half an hour to get dressed.
>
> Reflection on the Southern Ocean: windy, cold, icebergs everywhere, dangerous and extreme. Global warming is alive and well — there's something seriously wrong.

Team News Corp's new recruit, Nigel King, marvelled at his first-ever sighting of Cape Horn. Other yachts saw some novel forms of celebration for Cape first-timers. On *djuice dragons* their resident nudist, Anthony 'Nocka' Nossiter, did as one would expect: he took a hike around the deck as bare as a newborn baby. *Amer Sports Too*'s foredeck crewmember, Liz

Wardley (who struggles to own a pair of shoes), went barefoot around the Cape until the cold forced her to revert to wearing her sea boots.

Frustration was being experienced elsewhere. Soon after rounding the Cape *ASSA ABLOY*'s skipper, Neal McDonald, had no option but to show true leadership and take a freezing swim in three-degree water to clear stubborn kelp from the keel. On *Tyco*, skipper Kevin Shoebridge told of a day he'd rather forget: 'It started with a blocked toilet yesterday. This was followed by 10 gallons of water coming in through a cockpit vent and landing on me in my bunk. Just after I had changed into my dry gear in the nav. station, five more gallons came in that hatch, so I was soaked again. To finish the day, I found my gear bag floating in the bilge mixed with a cup of diesel. I am looking forward to tomorrow; wonderful sport this, I couldn't think of anything else I'd rather be doing.'

Valentine's Day, 14 February arrived.

Lisa McDonald:

Day 19 — Happy Valentine's Day from the girls ... XO

It makes me laugh. These girls are some of the world's toughest female sailors who have just emerged from dodging icebergs at mock speeds in the depths of the Southern Ocean. Valentine's Day rolls around and one by one, as the emails from loved ones come in, they go soft as putty and for a brief moment collapse into a puddle of emotional mush.

It's the little things that make the world go round out here; our team has received little love notes from all corners of the world and as near as 400 nautical miles away (from other yachts). There is not often time to think of home, family or friends while racing, and knowing that they are there, following our every pace to the next port, is what keeps us going ...

Having left Cape Horn in their wake, the tacticians, navigators and weather analysts in each crew had to combine their talents to decide whether to leave the Falkland Islands to port or starboard on this final stretch to Rio. The majority decision was to go west, with only *djuice dragons* and *Amer Sports One* opting to leave the islands to port. Initially port seemed the best choice, but eventually the west won.

The peace and serenity of the pleasant conditions off the Falklands were suddenly shattered for the *Team News Corp* crew with a thunderous, head-splitting roar. The shocked crew couldn't decipher what was happening until, in an instant, two British airforce jets roared out of nowhere and passed over the yacht just above mast-height. They arced out to the west then came back for another flypast, this time radioing the yacht to say that the commander of the British forces on the Falkland Islands wished them well.

Off the Falklands, Alby Pratt faced a major task — putting Bart Simpson's head back together again. Bart's head, which was emblazoned across the top of the yacht's 300-square-metre spinnaker, had literally exploded when the spinnaker was shredded in strong winds in the Southern Ocean. The sail was considered irreparable and destined for the rubbish bin, but the patient's status was reconsidered when the weather forecast for the waters north of Cape Horn became apparent. Only the Bart spinnaker could supply maximum speed in the expected light winds. So Alby pulled out his sewing machine, needle, bobbins and thread and started to sew in what was to become a marathon operation. Ross reported: 'There are just acres of cloth crammed in a tiny space. I marvel at the efforts the sail guys make. It's taken Alby 12 hours, but Bart's now back in one piece. It's not a pretty sight, though, because we've had to chop a little bit out of his head. He's not looking too good.'

Team News Corp was continuing to march on the leaders — the decision to gain leverage away from the fleet to the west was paying off. This, combined with the developing weather pattern, saw them perfectly placed to roll over the top of the boats ahead. Third, second, even first place could go their way.

On Day 19 Ross was on the helm. He pulled on the wheel to correct the boat when there was a sickening, resounding 'bang!' Their world had come to an end. The rudder had broken off and drifted away. Expletives rang through the air as the crew rushed to contain the situation. When he heard the bang Ross wasn't sure what had happened — he thought that perhaps the rig had come down. Then he realised that he couldn't feel anything on either steering wheel and at that moment one of the crew yelled out to him that the rudder was gone. The boat rounded up into the wind and they could only watch while the spinnaker flogged itself to death.

Ross:

> ... We are devastated. We've got a great boat and crew, and we were in a good position to move up the fleet. That's ocean racing.
>
> But I must say I'm pissed off ... I can only surmise that it must have happened as a result of hitting the ice. It must have weakened the rudderpost; it became weaker with time and finally broke. If there's one consolation it was that we got around Cape Horn before it broke.

Jez said that it was like looking at a corpse in the water when the rudder blade surfaced and floated away.

Gordon Maguire:

> ... I was sitting at the back of the boat and just saw [the rudder] pop out behind the stern and drift away. The boat immediately rounded up into the wind, all the sails flapping, and we were out of control. It was totally shattering, but you don't actually have time to sit and say, 'Shit, our race is over.' It was a case of, 'We now have a crisis on our hands, all the sails are flapping, our brand new Code 3 spinnaker is shaking itself to bits. We need to get it down' ... Next we had to get the emergency rudder out, which took us at least 20 minutes to get organised and in place so we could get sailing again.
>
> Then we had to have a damage evaluation; we were no longer going to be in the first five. How far behind were the girls? Were they in a position to catch us? If they were we would have to push — sail the boat as fast as we could to stay ahead of them. We decided that they were

*close enough — only 370 miles behind — and that was
do-able for them, particularly as we went north where the
wind was going to get lighter. As it got lighter the boats
would concertina together.*

The emergency rudder was a small fin half the size of the normal rudder that fits onto the stern of the boat. The crew made a makeshift tiller using spare racing equipment. To have a hold on the tiller and to be able to steer, the helmsman had to sit on the cockpit floor in an extremely uncomfortable position at the very back of the yacht.

This rudder is designed only as a safety measure, just to enable a yacht to get to port in the event of the main rudder breaking. And because of the rudder's small size the yacht quickly goes out of balance — and immediately out of control — in almost every gust. The crew had to be on their toes for every moment. As soon as the wind reached 10 knots they would need to reef the mainsail to maintain directional stability. By the time they reached Rio de Janeiro, 1200 miles away, they would hoist the mainsail up and down like a blind more than 100 times! Only in the faintest of breezes might a spinnaker or big Code Zero headsail be contemplated.

Ross:

*We are continuing to race because we want the points.
It would be too easy just to give up, pull the pin, go into
Uruguay and wait for the new rudder to arrive so we can
sail up the coast to Rio. But no one on board has even
considered that. Everyone just wants to get to Rio and
secure sixth place. There is no hesitation about pushing
the boat. We want to beat the girls. This is a setback, but
we have the crew, the boat and the support to come back.
The guys are pushing hard still, making changes to make
the boat go faster.*

*...All is well now. We are in our usual racing
watch system and making good miles — who knows we
might even ...*

*Better go on deck. I have been banned from steering
again for the rest of this trip.*

Jez turned to the lessons of history to sum up succinctly the attitude aboard *Team News Corp*: '"Never give in, never give in, never give in," ... the nine famous words of Winston Churchill. We were never going to give in.'

_∆_

DESPITE THEIR HANDICAP the *Team News Corp* crew raced as hard as they did when things were at full throttle onboard. Every fraction of a knot they could gain would help them secure sixth place and a valuable additional point.

The wind remained light but they constantly reminded themselves that they were sailing into the tropics, a region notorious for black clouds that brought savage squalls. Each crewmember's senses had to be razor sharp, forever alert in case a squall hit the yacht and sent it out of control. *Amer Sports Too* was closing in on them and Rio was still a long way away.

Things were progressing as normally as possible until one afternoon, when they watched a heavy black cloud form overhead. This drama-filled leg from Auckland was going to become even more dramatic. According to Gordon Maguire, there was nothing spectacular about the cloud, except that it was a little lower than the others. Suddenly it started turning in a small, tight circle, faster and faster. Then a massive cone formed at the bottom of the cloud, just above the mast. They were right under a waterspout that was forming into a perfect cone. The crew could even see up through the cone to the white cloud above it. All Gordon could think was, 'Oh my God, we've already seen one of these things, and I don't want to see another one.' It just kept reaching down towards them.

'There was some panic on deck, of course, in case it hit us,' says Gordon. 'We had all the sails ready to drop. It hit the water about a boat-length to windward, sucked up this amazing cloud of water, then moved diagonally aft and across the back of the boat, maybe 20 feet away. Then, as quickly as it appeared, it disappeared. It just disintegrated, whirling back up into the cloud. In a matter of minutes it was all over.'

Emergency over, again.

Ross:

> Day 22 — Time is starting to drag. There's only so much trimming one can do. If the helm is overloaded we could break the emergency steering. At the moment we have 17 knots of wind and we're sailing with a small reaching headsail and two reefs in the mainsail. Compare this to sailing full steam ahead: we would have a full 3000 square feet spinnaker, staysail and full main.
>
> It's frustrating and we constantly have to check ourselves from pushing too hard. If the emergency steering breaks we would be 'up the creek without a paddle'.
>
> The helmsman has to sit on the cockpit floor, holding onto a long tiller. It's hard work. You can only last half an hour at a time. We're working on the boat during the day to shorten the work list in Rio. We're monitoring the progress of Amer Sports Too — at present we look safe from her. It's terrible looking at the battle going on ahead and trying not to think 'if only'. We were in a bloody good position before breaking the rudder.

Just when things started to look better and sixth place seemed secure, the emergency rudder mounts on the yacht's stern began to show signs that they were breaking loose. The only option was to reduce speed, or face the prospect of losing the steering altogether. Nigel King spent eight hours making the necessary repairs, pirating all sorts of bits and pieces from the boat to keep things together.

At the same time the other crewmembers set about creating a better steering system, coming up with an ingenious system of tying the tiller to the steering wheels. As a result they could control the boat more easily and monitor the trim of the boat while they drove.

Favourable weather then enabled *Team News Corp* to sail a knot faster than *Amer Sports Too*. They held a 253-mile buffer and, finally, sixth place was starting to look like being secure again. While that was satisfying, it was equally frustrating to see how things were unfolding ahead. The pack was closing in on *illbruck* and there would be a 'flap-off' — a drifting match — over the closing stages. *illbruck* would eventually win the leg, but the other places went upside down, which in turn helped *Team News Corp*'s position in the overall points tally at the end of the stage.

Just on six days after their rudder broke, on a grey evening punctuated with a steamy tropical drizzle, *Team News Corp* appeared at the horizon to the south of Rio. The silhouetted, craggy mountain peaks overlooking the city and the city lights that began winking on the shore as darkness settled were welcoming sights for the race-weary crew.

Sixth place was theirs — and well deserved after their display of determination and seamanship. They were placed fourth overall, but sitting three points from second place behind *Amer Sports One* and *ASSA ABLOY*. *illbruck* was leading on 29 points from *Amer Sports One* on 22, *ASSA ABLOY* 20, *News Corp* 19, *Tyco* 18, *djuice dragons* 17, *SEB* 12 and *Amer Sports Too* 7.

After crossing the finish line *Team News Corp* made its way ever so slowly into the marina, where, despite the rain, a small but supportive crowd was on hand to welcome the crew and recognise their great achievement in completing the leg. As the yacht pulled alongside the dock it did appear in the dim light of the evening that the figure of Bart Simpson on the side of the hull looked considerably more determined.

The crew stepped down onto the dock like soldiers returning from the front line. Jez, who could hardly walk, was suffering most. He had what is commonly referred to as 'trench foot' — a condition that comes from the lack of circulation in the feet as a result of being exposed to freezing temperatures. It is one stage away from frostbite.

Ross summed up what had been a heinous sailing experience in the Southern Ocean: 'On a scale of one to ten for danger it was ten. There was no doubt about it. I openly admit that I was seriously worried and, on occasions, really scared.'

Top Respite in Rio for *Team News Corp*'s Alby Pratt, Nigel King, Steve Cotton and Damian 'Shreda' Duke. They had sailed into port only minutes earlier after the long haul from Auckland.

Centre Some of the *Team News Corp* crew visit Rio's famous Christ the Redeemer shrine. *Left to right:* Craig 'Smiley' Smith, Alby Pratt, Jez Fanstone, Nigel King, Ian 'Barney' Walker and Gordon Maguire.

Bottom There's no rest for the shore crew when the yacht is in port. Jan van der Lee takes care of crew clothing.

All images *Richard Langdon/Ocean Images*

≪ *Team News Corp* cruises
past Rio's Copacabana Beach
with the giant Christ the
Redeemer statue high above.
Richard Langdon/Ocean Images

≫RIO DE JANEIRO
TO MIAMI

Pirates are always in the back of your mind.

LISA MCDONALD — SKIPPER, *AMER SPORTS TOO*

rio de Janeiro. The name conjures images of 'The Girl from Ipanema', Copacabana Beach, thumping parties and scantily clad women gyrating their way through the city during the legendary Carnival.

For the Volvo race crews and their supporters it was all of that for the stopover, but there were many who were not sad to see the city disappearing in the wake as the fleet headed off on the 4450-mile fifth stage to Miami. Despite the appearance of a grandiose past, with its majestic buildings and magnificent beachfront esplanade, much of Rio is desperately poor today, and for many of its citizens crime is the only way to survive.

Among those who faced the terrifying experience of being robbed at knifepoint by one of the bands of unruly youths prowling the strip along Copacabana Beach were Jez's wife, Leah, Ashley Abbott and her husband, John. They had been out for dinner and had decided to take a walk along the beach opposite their hotel. The beach was well lit by spotlights and they noticed in the distance a group of young guys sitting on the sand near the water's edge. One of the youths started walking towards them, so they decided to turn around and head back to the hotel, but as they did Ashley noticed that the youth was holding a knife under his arm. She called to John and Leah to stay close, then suddenly the mob approached them. The first guy pulled the knife and held it at John's throat. One of the others grabbed Leah. Terrified, Ashley let out an earsplitting scream. It worked. The attackers were startled, which gave John the split second needed to fumble his way into his pocket, pull out some Brazilian money and give it to them. As they ran off, they ripped Ashley's watch from her wrist while Leah, who had wrestled with the guy attacking her, surrendered her necklace. The three ran to the edge of the esplanade, where they stopped and looked at each other, speechless, and in shock. Crossing to the middle of the esplanade, they told a group of on-duty police what had just happened. The police shrugged their shoulders and told them in fractured English not to go near the beach at night.

Team News Corp helmsman Barney Walker was another victim, but in less threatening circumstances. Two women befriended him on the esplanade and, before he knew it, the cash in his pocket had disappeared. Other sailors were also robbed.

The teams also had to contend with an outbreak of the debilitating mosquito-borne dengue fever, a by-product of Brazil's stifling tropical climate, where the humidity tried its hardest to exceed 100 per cent.

But there were plus sides: spectacular scenery and wonderful hospitality — especially at the dockside Caipirinha Party, where thirsty crews and supporters consumed 40 litres of the seemingly toxic concoction before someone went into an uncontrollable spin during the body-sliding contest across the wet floor. The manoeuvre took out the main support for the lightweight roof in what was a temporary bar. The plastic sheeting came down like a stack of cards and the party came to an end.

It was near time to leave Rio and head for Miami.

TEAM NEWS CORP was out of the water for four days during the stopover so the replacement rudder, which had been airfreighted from England, could be prepared and fitted. As the yacht came out of the water, dangling precariously from the end of a huge mobile crane, the only evidence of a rudder were shreds of carbon fibre hanging like black string from what remained of the thick rudderpost. There was no real clue as to what had caused it to break. The Southern Ocean iceberg remained the likely culprit.

When Jeff Scott left to go back home to his family, a more than adequate replacement was found in Matt Humphries, a 30-year-old Englishman doing his fourth race around the world. He had quit *Team SEB* to join *Team News Corp*. Ross and Jez decided that Nick would step off the boat for the leg — Australian Peter 'Spike' Doriean, who had left the *djuice* campaign, was his replacement in the 12-man crew. Matt would become a helmsman and help with on-deck tactics, Spike would be a sail trimmer and Ross and Steve Cotton would combine forces for the meteorology work and navigation below deck. These types of adjustments were fairly typical — many of the teams changed crews regularly as the race advanced.

With more than half the total points still up for grabs on the remaining five legs, Germany's *illbruck* held a satisfying seven-point advantage over Grant Dalton's *Amer Sports One* going into this leg. But it wasn't a comfortable second place for *Amer* because just two points behind, on a total score of 20, was *ASSA ABLOY*. The next three teams had just two points separating them — *Team News Corp* 19 points, *Tyco* 18 and *djuice* 17. The 4450-mile leg that would take the fleet back into the northern hemisphere was expected to be primarily a trade wind sleigh-ride, with some tricky bits near the start and finish and the massive meteorological hurdle of the equatorial doldrums in the middle. It sounded relatively easy, but the level of competitiveness already displayed among the fleet on this round-the-world odyssey meant that one tactical error, poor sail selection or the wrong analysis of the weather would prove very expensive.

Conditions for the start were typical of the sultry tropical climate, with the wind very soft and constantly switching direction. It was anyone's guess who would weave their way to the front on the 50-mile upwind leg to Cabo Frio, where it was a left turn towards the equator. First *Amer Sports One*, then *Tyco*, then *djuice*, took the lead. Then it went back the other way. But it was close racing, in fact, too close for *Team SEB* and *illbruck*. The helmsman on *SEB*, which was sailing on port tack, misjudged the ducking manoeuvre they planned for going behind *illbruck*. BANG! Travelling at around 8 knots, *SEB* did a bow-plant into *illbruck*'s port side just near the transom, ripping out a stanchion and punching a fist-sized hole into the side of the boat. The *SEB* crew, recognising they were at fault, immediately turned their yacht through a 720-degree penalty turn to exonerate themselves, as per the race rules.

The fleet headed offshore on port tack, looking for the time to turn onto starboard and benefit from the lift that would come from a high-pressure system that had developed out in the Atlantic. Deciding just when to tack would be crucial for the stretch up the coast of Brazil.

Team News Corp, which had a shocker of a start by finding every light patch and unfavourable change in wind direction, got this part of the race spot-on. They tacked to the north first, well before the others, and within the first two days of what would be a 19-day race they had established a significant lead.

Ross:

Day 3 — Shocking start, but we got away without any problems. We were the last to round the first corner, Cabo Frio, but then, to our surprise, no one else in the fleet took the inside and we have bounced to first. Right at the moment we have a nice counter-current pushing us towards the top of South America. We feel comfortable where we are, but time will tell. It's going to be a very interesting sked in three hours' time — to see if any of the fleet has split.

It's great to be back at sea, in clean air, clean water and no noise. It's hot and sunny at the moment. Downstairs is like an oven, whilst on deck it's cool with a nice breeze . . .

Team News Corp had a great lead, more than 20 miles — a massive margin after three days of racing. But then, to use the words of more than one crewmember, they blew it. Instead of consolidating, cashing in on their profit by going back and covering the opposition, they looked for far greater gains. It was a speculative deal that would backfire.

Jez:

We should have consolidated and gone back to the fleet when we could have . . . and still been in front. There was discussion at the time about going back to cover . . . we stayed closer to the shore while the better breeze was offshore. One morning we were pretty much parked for about eight hours and that was it. The others rolled us.

The soul-destroying tactical blunder sent *Team News Corp* spiralling from first to fifth and from that moment it was a case of playing a serious game of catch-up. *illbruck*, *Tyco*, *ASSA ABLOY* and *Amer Sports One* were filling the major places and, by staying in contact with each other and match racing, were building a strong barrier between themselves and their pursuers. There was soul searching aboard *Team News Corp*. Major lessons were being learned. And, as if copping the cake in the face wasn't enough, there was another very undesirable problem onboard.

Ross:

Twelve sweaty bodies on a 60-foot boat is not a nice smell. During the day no one sleeps. You lie on your bunk with the sweat pouring out of you. You try not to move because that causes more sweating. You look forward to the night time because it's cooler and down below is just OK. Remember, there is no chance to have an ice drink or a cool salad. The drinking water is warm and we are still eating hot food. All the crew agree on one thing, though: we'd rather be hot than freezing cold in the Southern Ocean.

On a lighter note (I should say smelly note), not only are the bodies of the crew beginning to smell in the heat but so are some of the sail bags. A Brazilian cat obviously decided that some of our sail bags were his/her territory, so laid claim by peeing on them. As you can imagine, as the boat heats up the smell gets worse. I can imagine that every Miami cat will be down to welcome us in and try to lay claim to the sails.

Any advice on how to get rid of the smell would be appreciated.

The *Team News Corp* website was soon overflowing with ideas on how to eradicate the smell of cat pee. Sadly for the crew, the race yacht carried none of the products suggested, so the stench became an even more undesirable feature of the leg.

Up ahead *ASSA ABLOY*, which had moved into the lead, *illbruck* and *Tyco* were having a 'knock 'em down, drag 'em out' stoush.

Stu Bannatyne — watch leader, *illbruck*:

What a day it has been — the closest ocean racing, as we have the whole fleet within 20 miles and in our own piece of water we have been dicing with ASSA ABLOY and Tyco all day. Never before at this stage in a leg have we had to be so concerned about keeping our air clear. This morning we had ASSA ABLOY camp on us and block our every move from 20 degrees below course to 30 degrees above. They were determined not to give us any quarter. It was a bit odd really, because we both lost a lot on all the other boats as they covered our every move. Eventually we slipped past them, anyway, so it was all a waste of time for them. One wonders if someone onboard has a personal vendetta against us? Six hours later, the situation repeated itself. ASSA ABLOY managed to ride a squall over our bow and is now a few hundred metres ahead once more. Here we go again for the night, a close race as we try to make the most of every rain squall that comes our way.

Apart from stiff competition this was a leg of obstacles for all the yachts — unlit native fishing boats at night, oil rigs, cargo ships, being 'slimed' by kamikaze flying fish, and off the northern coast of South America ... possibly pirates!

Stig Westergaard — trimmer/helmsman, *djuice dragons*:
You can look for a lot of other 'things' in Rio, safety not being one of them. I got mugged ... I contributed to the social welfare of Brazil by kindly donating my watch to five hustlers. Off we go to find safety at sea. Yeah, right. We are now approaching some of the most notorious piracy waters in the world. Luckily, we're sailing in convoy ...

Eyes were forever scanning the horizon as the yachts weaved their way through the various obstructions. Imagine, though, what it was like being on the other side of the fence: ambling along on your cruising yacht in a remote part of the planet ...

Rodney Ardern — watch leader, *SEB*:

In the last 24 hours we have had a few close encounters
with the locals. During the night we had to avoid a poorly
lit cruising catamaran that was idling along with not a
care in the world ... only to be rudely disrupted by six
screaming yachties politely explaining the intricacies of
the right-of-way rules. Is that the pot calling the kettle
black [after the incident with illbruck]?

We were stunned to see the state of the local sailing
canoes out today — very low freeboard, simple main and
jib and a versatile rig — heavily raked going upwind and
over the bow downwind. Either these guys are closely
following the America's Cup trends in Auckland or we
have 100 years of sailing lessons to learn from the locals.

Lisa McDonald — skipper, *Amer Sports Too*:

A strange thing happened tonight. We came upon a small
ship that didn't show up on radar until we were almost
abeam of it. I guess we were lucky it was well lit up — we
just sailed around it. It must have been made of banana
leaves and not carrying a radar reflector. So now we know
it's not just the little fishing boats that may not show up
on the screen, but big ones, too. We started talking about
pirates, which are always in the back of your mind,
especially near unknown coastal areas.

Stories about experiences with the locals flowed for days. In particular, the
seafaring prowess of the fishermen impressed the round-the-world sailors.

Richard Clarke — helmsman/trimmer, *illbruck*:

Had some close encounters with many of the locals today,
as the fishing fleet was out in full force. We narrowly
missed five small fishing boats and we were close enough
to almost sample the catch of the day. You should have

seen the little boats these guys are in. We are about 25 miles off the coast and there are three guys in a 15-foot boat pulling in their catch by hand. The boats have no engines and are powered only by a small sail. We went by them in the early hours: either they got a very early start or they spent the night out there. I wonder what they must think of eight state-of-the-art sail boats blasting by them, heading for places they don't know. Maybe they are envious of all the fish they might be able to catch sailing the waters of the world in a VO 60.

IN LIGHT-WEATHER RACING in particular, weight is critical to speed. Nothing superfluous is allowed onboard and the volume of the necessities is carefully calculated. When it comes to fuel it's a bit like Formula One motor racing — you want to use the last drop just as you reach the finish. Aboard *Team News Corp*, however, it was starting to look as though the sums weren't adding up.

Ross:

> *Day 7 — A crisis looming — do we have enough fuel? With all the water ballasting [water pumped in and out by using the auxiliary engine], battery charging, making of drinking water and using small fans inside the boat to cool us down, it appears that we have slightly underestimated our fuel supplies to run the generator. With the increased consumption of drinking water and the fans, we are now using the same amount of fuel we used in the Southern Ocean when we had heaters on. Plans have been put into place to ensure that we're OK.*
>
> *Life onboard is still steaming hot during the day. The water temperature on our instruments shows 30 degrees Celsius, which is the same as the air temperature on an*

*extremely hot day in New Zealand. Making coffee is easy:
the water takes about one minute to boil. We all look
forward to those beautiful cool nights.*

THE PRESSURE OF playing the catch-up game aboard *Team News Corp*
continued, yet with thousands of miles to go they still weren't out of the race
as they approached the doldrums. They were in fourth spot, only 30 miles
off the lead, and they held a 20-mile advantage over *djuice*. Still, the decision
onboard was to go on a tangent and try to burst through the doldrums
better than anyone else. It was another gamble.

Gordon Maguire:

> *If we'd just followed the others through the gap, we
> probably would have caught the leading group ... but we
> didn't and that gave them a 200-mile lead and dropped
> us to last. To a certain extent, for me anyway, that was
> the straw that broke the camel's back in terms of: 'We've
> obviously got our strategy wrong here, guys; we're going
> all the way out to the left, all out to the right, all out to
> the left again and sailing ourselves into last place.'*

There was some light relief, albeit brief, for a team that was again trying
to recover from an ongoing run of outs. Nigel King was the only equator
virgin aboard *News Corp*, so he had the entire crew stacked against him. The
most enthusiastic of his assailants was Irishman Justin Slattery, who, with
great gusto, shaved off one of Nigel's eyebrows. Someone suggested this was
payback for 400 years of English oppression, rather than Nigel's induction
into the equator-crossing club.

Halfway through the leg Lisa McDonald and her crew were sailing
brilliantly. The light wind conditions meant the physical demands on the
crew were less, and that suited them. Through some clever tactics and a

display of great mettle they were causing embarrassment for many of their male rivals. *Amer Sports Too* had sailed into fifth place, leaving in their wake their 'boss' Grant Dalton aboard *Amer Sports One*, *Team News Corp* and *djuice*. Lisa's husband Neal sent a message of congratulations from *ASSA ABLOY*, while *djuice*'s skipper, Knut Frostad, emailed: 'Good on you girls. Keep it up. We cross our fingers that you beat one of the skippers (no names mentioned) who once claimed that if ever he was beaten by the girls he would walk naked up the main street of Auckland with a pineapple up his ****.' The identity of the unnamed skipper would be revealed at the end of the race when the girls did what was required of them — beat him home.

Ross:

> *Day 9 — Been one of those days. Lost big miles and have, yet again, attracted every black cloud. It started raining six hours ago and hasn't stopped since — reminds me of summer in Auckland. Welcome to the doldrums ... we thought we had passed through them a few hundred miles ago, but at the time I was slightly suspicious that they weren't the real thing — it was too easy. We are definitely in them now — rain, lightning, huge gusts of wind from any direction, black clouds everywhere, but we are nearly out of them. The breeze is becoming steadier in direction and strength and the clouds are clearing.*
>
> *I hope the others have been hit as hard as us. Is our little bit of leverage on the fleet going to pay? I believe so — it will give us a nice angle to head into the island of Barbuda, which is still 1680 miles away.*
>
> *The rain has cooled the air, thank goodness, but we still have the hatches open to keep the inside cool. Of course, the rain pours inside, but we just keep emptying it out.*
>
> *Looking for the better sked in 35 minutes, but in the meantime we continue to change sails every 10 minutes or so. The foredeck looks like a 'Chinese laundry', with sails all over the place waiting to be hoisted.*

That much-anticipated sked brought more gloom for the *Team News Corp* crew. It finally confirmed that the circuitous route they had opted to take through the doldrums was yet another costly mistake. They were then more than 100 miles off the lead and worse was to come.

If there was a bright side, though, it was that the fleet was now back in the northern hemisphere for the first time in six months. That meant refreshing trade winds would soon be powering them north past the Caribbean islands of the West Indies, the Bahamas and into Miami.

When the trade winds arrived it was sailing at its finest — a northeasterly breeze of between 18 and 20 knots that allowed the yachts to power reach under masthead spinnaker at speeds of up to 15 knots. With these conditions the race became a procession — there were few, if any, passing lanes available where tactical moves could be made. Every mile gained on the others was a hard gain.

This didn't, however, stop the *illbruck* crew from surging forward. These tight reaching conditions proved yet again how fast the German entry was sailing across the wind. In a matter of hours John Kostecki and his team had established a 12-mile lead over second-placed *ASSA ABLOY*. *Tyco* was three miles further astern and then there was a huge gap — more than 80 miles — to fourth-placed *Team SEB*. *Team News Corp* was languishing in seventh place, almost 170 miles down *illbruck*'s wake. Warm winds, warm water, relatively smooth seas ... the dreams of sailors were being realised, as Jason Carrington reported from *ASSA ABLOY*: 'Life on deck simply does not get any better than this. There's even time for a laugh as a flying fish hits trimmer Richard Mason clean on the chin.'

Steve Hayles — navigator, *Tyco*:

Despite being a good evening for us on Tyco *it has not been a good day for Nipper (aka Guy Salter) who had a flying fish ordeal of a different kind. The normal problem with these winged wonders from the deep is that prior to take off it seems they don't do very good pre-flight checks and often find a VO60 or, more specifically, a crewmember on a VO60, in their flight path. Having either landed on the deck or incapacitated a member of the crew, we normally throw them over the side for humanitarian reasons (plus they make a major mess of the decks). Nipper's problem was that one flew completely unnoticed into a sail bag (days earlier) which was right at the back of the boat. When the call came to peel [change] that sail today he ended up covered in the stinking remains ... It was getting dark and the breeze was up, so it was not the ideal time for a saltwater shower, but there was no way we were letting him down below before several gallons of water had been used to get rid of the smell. He retired to his bunk well after the rest of his watch, cold and a little shaken by the experience.*

But the best flying fish episode on this leg — a real 'believe it or not' story — came from *Team SEB*. It was good enough to put all other flying fish stories to rest.

Scott Beavis — bowman, *Team SEB*:
Sailing along peacefully in about 8 to 9 knots of breeze under full main and Code Zero, Glen went to fill one of the ballast tanks. He went through the same procedure he had performed a thousand times before: turn the generator on, open the thru-hull valve, open the horizontal transfer valve, select a tank, open the tank face valve and turn on the ballast pump. This time the system made an odd sound as he switched on the ballast pump, almost as if something was stuck in the thru-hull valve. He stopped the pump, closed the valve, opened the valve and started the pump. This time the tank filled, no worries. About 15 minutes later, a crewmember spotted something silver shimmering inside the tank through one of the inspection ports. His intuitive nature led him to open the inspection port. Believe it or not, a flying fish, looking slightly worse for

wear (after going through the ballast system) was swimming around. I could tell you it flew out of the tank, out the hatch and back into the ocean, but that would be stretching the truth a little too far ...

—))

FINALLY THERE WAS some good news for *Team News Corp*: they had brought one of the opposition into their sights. At last they could confirm that they were making gains on the fleet.

Ross:

> *Day 14 — At sun-up, right on our bow was* Amer Sports One, *a great sight as this is the first boat we have seen since we split from the fleet outside Rio. Looking forward to the match race ... Since first sighting* Amer Sports One *we have made gains by climbing up onto her hip and slowly rolling over the top.*
>
> *We have had a minor crisis onboard. Barney decided to wash the dishes after dinner last night. This, in itself, was a major step forward for Barney — he isn't often seen around the galley area, other than raiding the food bags. Anyway, in this washing up he has lost three of our eating spoons. This may not sound like a crisis, but we only have six spoons onboard to start with and these are used for eating, stirring coffee, etc.*
>
> *The boat's been turned upside down but, finally, under heavy interrogation, he admitted that they may have (note the 'may have') been in the bottom of the pot when he emptied the waste over the side. The result is that we have scaled down our search, Barney has been banned from the galley, and the off-watch, who eat before coming on deck, have to be woken earlier to give*

them time to eat their meal sharing the three spoons and
still get on deck in time.

When you are racing around the world you must expect plenty of things to happen — but not being attacked by an unidentified ocean object. *ASSA ABLOY*'s navigator, Mark Rudiger, reported just that. Crewmembers looked astern to see something cutting an erratic swathe of white across the surface towards them. There was mild panic until someone realised that they had hooked the float line of a lobster pot around the keel and the pot was being dragged along behind. For *Amer Sports One* dolphins doing aerobatics provided entertainment during this downhill trade wind slide.

Jeff Brock — bowman, *Amer Sports One*:

I have seen a lot of dolphins in my time, but never with so much vertical pace. These boys had some serious fun, and wanted us to see every bit of it. I could honestly say 30 feet might have been the record of the launch-fest with a beautiful back floppy and a crazy tail wiggle to finish.

A humpback was aiming to please as well. She could not quite get her tail out of the water ... but tried her best. Spotted by Freddy Loof [mid-deck crew] on our windward quarter, just 300 feet away, a 50-foot humper breached for joy. I say she was horny, and looking for action; Freddy says she was just plain itchy and had to have a scratch. In response Pete Pendleton [yacht systems manager] said, 'That's the same thing, knucklehead.'

By now the *Team News Corp* crew had resigned themselves to the fact that this was going to be an expensive leg. The trade winds were holding and there was no chance of making any real impression on the leaders. *illbruck* was still in front, 125 miles closer to Miami. The challenge now was to claim *Amer Sports One*, which was just five miles ahead, and move into fifth place. There was also a chance *SEB* could be claimed ... if there was sufficient runway left.

Alby Pratt:

Day 15 — The perfect sailing conditions continue for Team News Corp, with steady breeze from behind and our biggest spinnaker up. The only disadvantage we have is that being at latitude 19 degrees north, the sun is very high in the sky and conditions on deck are absolutely roasting. The sails aren't offering any shade whatsoever with the sun so high, and the watch on deck can feel themselves getting slowly cooked alive as the temperature tops out at 43 degrees Celsius in the afternoon.

The intense heat combined with the constant exposure to salt water is causing most of the crew to break out in small boils where their clothing chafes their skin. Some guys have it so badly that they are taking antibiotics to prevent infection setting in. Sunburn is also a major issue and we seem to be churning through the suncream as we try to keep the melanomas at bay. The only respite from the heat is the occasional bucket of salt water, which we throw over ourselves, but this soon dries off, leaving the itchy salt behind and more aggravation for the boils. Some guys think it is better just to sweat it out. I'm not sure which is the better option.

We received an email yesterday with some news about an iceberg the size of Rhode Island breaking off Antarctica. Those freezing conditions we were in the thick of down there, only eight weeks ago, now seem like another life as we head to Miami.

Team News Corp and Amer Sports One had found their way ahead of Lisa McDonald's team when Amer Sports One received an unexpected blast from the heavens: the yacht was struck by lightning while sailing under a cloud full of torrential rain. No-one was injured and the yacht was not damaged, but the strike blew out almost every electrical instrument onboard.

ON THE 18TH day of racing, when the fleet was surging past the islands of the Bahamas, all of a sudden it appeared that something was wrong with *illbruck*. *ASSA ABLOY* and *Tyco* were closing fast. The reason for this rapid gain was soon revealed — the *illbruck* crew had seen their massive gennaker (spinnaker) get ripped to shreds in a gust of wind. They were wounded, as this was the ultimate sail for the downwind conditions they were experiencing. It was now looking as though their lead of more than 30 miles would not be enough to stay ahead of the challengers before reaching the finish.

In little more than a day *ASSA ABLOY* was showing the way to Miami, but with conditions becoming lighter on the approach, victory was still far from assured. Just one hour from the finish line *ASSA ABLOY* almost came to a halt in near-windless conditions and *illbruck* and *Tyco* continued to make ground. But there was enough puff for *ASSA ABLOY* to secure first. *illbruck* and *Tyco*, which both found the same light conditions near Miami, finished within 75 minutes of the winner. *Team News Corp* did claim *Amer Sports One* and finish fifth, 70 minutes astern of fourth-placed *SEB* and five hours off the winner's pace. For *Team News Corp* it was time to reflect on what had been the most disappointing leg so far.

Gordon Maguire:

> *Everybody else in the fleet seems to understand this, and it's now been beaten into us ... the first four boats stayed together, raced all the way around and they finished one, two, three, and four. They hardly deviated more than 4 or 5 miles from each other's line. We, on the other hand, were 100 miles out to one side hoping for a miracle, and it didn't come.*

Jez:

> *We fired our ammunition and hit the target early, but forgot to reload.*

For Ross it was time to get off the boat. He stated that he and Steve Cotton had 'stuffed up' the navigation and tactical decisions on the leg. More importantly, though, he couldn't continue sailing because his back problems were recurring to such a degree that he would probably require surgery. Steve was so frustrated by the circumstances surrounding the result that he resigned and returned to New Zealand.

Top A disappointing result didn't stop the champagne from flowing when *Team News Corp* arrived in Miami. *Rick Tomlinson*

Centre A crowded day in the office. Sailing and shore crew work below deck in Miami.
Richard Langdon/Ocean Images

Bottom Tethered thoroughbreds. The VOR fleet is ready to be unleashed for the race from Miami to Baltimore. *Rick Tomlinson*

≪ With a huge task ahead of it, *Team News Corp* sets out in pursuit of the fleet following the controversial recall back to the start line in Miami.

Richard Langdon/Ocean Images

MIAMI TO BALTIMORE

Know your enemy, otherwise you die.

GORDON MAGUIRE — WATCH LEADER, *TEAM NEWS CORP*

LEG SIX

the Rio de Janeiro to Miami leg delivered a massive wake-up call for *Team News Corp*, so the crew changes came as no surprise to team members or outside observers. Ross's decision to retire from the racing crew and fly to London for medical advice on his damaged back was inevitable. But the 53-year-old's disappointment at being grounded was far outweighed by some very personal satisfaction — his partner of nine years (and *Team News Corp*'s nutritionist), Jan van der Lee, accepted his proposal of marriage. 'I didn't get down on my knees to propose,' said Ross. 'I couldn't — my back was too sore. Thank God Jan's so understanding...'

With Ross and Steve gone, the crew had to be restructured. Jez returned to being sole skipper, Nick White rejoined the crew as meteorologist and Stuart Childerley, England's world Etchells class and ocean racing champion, joined as a helmsman. Matt Humphries moved from being a back-up helmsman to tactical navigator. They were a formidable team who, following the debacle of the previous leg, would leave the dock in Miami more determined than ever to impress on the 875-mile dash north to Baltimore.

Just prior to departure on 14 April Gordon Maguire recalled some words from a book written by a Chinese philosopher about the art of war: 'Rule number one was "Know your enemy, otherwise you die". We had trouble on the previous two legs because we didn't sail with the enemy, so we weren't able to get to know much about them. The game plan for this leg is to stay with the leaders and try to pass them with superior sailing skills and boat speed. The most intelligent ocean racers in the world are out there and to think that we know better than them is probably the most arrogant thing we could do.'

The key influence on the leg would be the Gulf Stream, the river of warm water that sweeps out of the Gulf of Mexico and northwards along the east coast of America before bending out into the Atlantic near Cape Hatteras and dissipating as it heads towards Europe. It is a conveyor belt that can increase a boat's speed by up to three knots.

According to the history of the race, this would probably be a light weather leg; light trade winds prevailing in the south, then a mixed bag to the north. The warm, moist air accompanying the Gulf Stream can have a significant influence on the weather pattern — major, violent storms can result when it merges with the dry, hot air of the continental landmass. Negotiating a path around these storms to encounter the most favourable winds is a critical requirement. And the final 120 miles of the leg up the wide expanse of Chesapeake Bay to Baltimore can be a real lottery. Constant vigilance of changing weather patterns and harnessing every opportunity almost always provides the winning break.

Heavy rain lashed the dock at Miami Marina as the teams prepared to depart for the race start area; not that there was much activity. The hardy crowd of spectators who turned up to farewell the crews were beginning to wonder if they were at the right venue. Few racing sailors could be seen — most of them were sitting below deck doing their best to stay dry as long as possible.

They reappeared when it was time to leave, each yacht's cue to drop the dock lines being the blast of its battle song over the marina's PA system. *ASSA ABLOY*'s departure was the most popular, with the high-kicking Miami High School cheerleaders doing a 'Thank you Miami' dance routine on the foredeck.

As the yachts paraded down the Government Cut channel towards the open sea the passengers aboard one of the world's largest cruise liners waved and cheered from their high-altitude vantage point. They were probably trying to comprehend how vessels so seemingly small could master the world's oceans, especially when compared with the massive proportions of their five-star floating hotel. The farewell became warmer a little later when the clouds changed their complexion and began to clear. Soon the sun was baking the coastal beaches and Miami began to look a little more like what you see in the brochures.

Once outside the channel and clear of the rocky breakwater, the yachts turned north and cruised across a gentle ocean swell to the starting zone four miles away. The area was easily identified by the flotilla of sail boats and powerboats that had gathered to see the battle. These spectators were to get far more than they bargained for — this was to be the most memorable start of the six to date, for all the wrong reasons. In the minutes before the start gun all yachts did runs timed towards the line to calculate the influence of the Gulf Stream. With the trade wind wafting in from the southeast at around 15 knots it would be a downwind start; spinnakers would be set, and with the 'stream' providing an additional two knots of speed the possibility of a premature start was very real. It was going to be tricky.

The start signal sounded and for the supporters of *Team News Corp* it was the dream getaway. The spinnaker was up and drawing superbly right on the gun. 'Bluey', as the boat was now referred to, was leaving the rest of the fleet in its wide, white wake. Cheers went up — but soon the elation turned to disbelief. Six of the eight yachts were declared premature starters by officials on the start boat and recalled to the line to start again. The McDonald family, Neal and Lisa, were the only ones to get it right: *ASSA ABLOY* and *Amer Sports Too* were given the 'all-clear'. It proved to be a time-consuming breach for *Team News Corp* because they were the most distant from the line when called back — Bluey took longer than any other to return, start correctly and resume racing. Jez accepted the punishment but some of the crew, including helmsman Barney Walker and Gordon Maguire, who was steering at the time, weren't happy with the way the Race Committee handled the situation.

Barney:

> I don't think we broke the start but, regardless, we looked
> for a plus in the situation. What came to mind was that
> the last time I broke a start and had to go back was in the
> Sydney to Hobart race, and we ended up winning the
> race. So I said to Gordon, 'Don't worry, mate. The last
> time I broke the start we won the yacht race. It's an omen.'

If it was an omen its influence started working very quickly. After being the last yacht to restart and lagging more than 2 miles behind the leaders, *Team News Corp* was soon charging back into contention. By the time the yacht reached the end of the spectator boat exclusion zone just 5 miles up the coast they had already caught *djuice dragons* and had *Team SEB* and *Tyco* in their sights. Within two hours *Tyco* was astern and by nightfall they were level with *SEB*. It was the incentive they needed to press even harder. They were applying their 'stay in touch and beat them with superior speed and tactics' attitude, and with the wind already going soft, two decisions they'd made prior to the start were already paying off: a new light-weather Code 1 spinnaker created by Alby was proving lethal, plus Nick's heavily researched forecast for light winds had seen them start the race with the boat as light as possible. The decision was to carry fewer sails, reduce the amount of food onboard — because no one would starve on such a short leg — limit the contents of the tool kit and restrict the amount of clothing each crewmember carried. The weight loss program had eliminated nearly 250 kilograms of 'excess baggage'. It was like leaving three crewmembers ashore.

While the light downwind conditions placed no real physical demands on the teams — except during sail changes — the first night was psychologically draining. The crew that could maintain maximum concentration, exploit every wind shift and grab every tactical opportunity would do the best.

Barney:

> On average we were doing two spinnaker changes every four-hour watch just to keep the boat sailing at maximum speed. The wind was shifting between 40 and 50 degrees, so the staysail was also going up and down as required. It was really tough trying to stay in touch with the other boats — with so many wind shifts they were spearing off on courses that varied by 20 or 30 degrees. We had to decide who we thought was doing the right thing and go with them, but at the same time we had to keep our game plan in mind — we had to be on the east side of the fleet when thunderstorms were forming between the Gulf Stream and the coast. That plan proved correct because any boat that sagged off to our left, west towards the coast, lost out big-time. Basically, the thunderstorms chewed up the wind. We held better pressure out to sea.

Nick White was continually monitoring the weather and plotting the course. He also took time out to consider life as a Volvo race competitor and what lay ahead when he rejoined Dennis Conner's America's Cup campaign in Auckland as a meteorologist. 'What a great morning,' he wrote in an email. 'It is sunny and we are reaching along with the spinnaker up. It has been great to come back onboard for this leg. In this racing we get dawns at sea and not a wake-up call at 5am to go to the gym. Officially we've picked off another boat — *Amer Sports One* — and moved up to third place, but in reality they are just off our beam. The girls are way out to the right and we are just right of the main bunch, which is where we want to be. Hopefully our positioning will pay off as the breeze changes direction. The boat seems strangely quiet without Ross. We all hope he gets well soon.'

That night the international media release from the VOR office confirmed the right-hand side of the course to be the best; satellite plotting had *Team News Corp* placed first, albeit by the narrowest of margins. Nick was quite unassuming about the achievement. 'It's quite a good feeling to be leading. We seem to have a slight edge in speed on most of the other boats — which definitely helps — and we seem to have found the best part of the ocean to sail in.' The difficult part would be to maintain their lead all the way to the Chesapeake. The crew quietly got on with the job of capitalising on the benefits of the Gulf Stream against the breeze, which was slowly changing direction in their favour.

Relentless concentration was the key. It was essential for everyone on the watch to sail the yacht to its target speed while maintaining optimum wind angles on the desired course. At the same time they had to stay in contact with the opposition, which was relatively easy because the other frontrunners, *illbruck*, *ASSA ABLOY*, and *Tyco*, were so close. Every 15 minutes Matt and Nick checked the radar and gave the crew updates on gains and losses. The racing was so tight that these margins were measured in boat lengths. Little had changed by Day 4. These masters of the world's oceans were playing one of the most intense games of aquatic chess imaginable. The only difference was that there were now three contenders left in the fight for first. *ASSA ABLOY* had made a tactical blunder by splitting from the pack and had fallen more than 20 miles behind.

Navigator Mark Rudiger explained in an email from *ASSA ABLOY* that beyond the bad move it had not been a good day all round. A large amount of weed had caught on the keel and propeller strut on two occasions so they'd had to send a man overboard each time to clear it. They had also found unfavourable wind and current conditions and, to top it all off ... 'Yours truly accidentally hit the wrong switch in the dark with the generator running, exploded a water ballast line and almost sank the boat!'

Rudiger also decided it was time to throw a little controversy into the ring by commenting on Grant Dalton's ongoing claims that his yacht, *Amer Sports One*, was slow: 'Dalton has been on a crusade for some reason against Frers (the designer) and what a slow boat he designed. I doubt many of us out here or the media buy the propaganda or understand why he says it. The fact is that *Amer Sports One* has repeatedly sailed from behind up to the leaders and often right past them. They did this again yesterday. There is nothing wrong with their boat speed when compared to any other boat in the fleet: they all have strengths and weaknesses. When *Amer Sports One* is in the right place and has the right sail up, they do just fine.' The comments did not prompt a response from Dalton or his team.

The lighter-than-ever *News Corp* was romping along, maintaining a one-mile advantage over *illbruck*, with another mile to *Amer Sports One*. The crew were happy to have the opposition so close in such fickle wind conditions. It gave them a better opportunity to counter every move the other yachts made.

Matt Humphries:

> As I sit in the nav. station the winches above me constantly groan as the trimmers work every wind shift and gust. It's been extremely pleasant running under spinnaker up the Gulf Stream. Four years ago on this leg we were slamming to windward — 30 knots of wind against current — which was, to say the least, very unpleasant. Currently we have the edge over our nearest rivals, illbruck, Amer Sports One *and* ASSA ABLOY, *but we are only too aware that this could change as we battle our way to Cape Hatteras and then onto Chesapeake Bay. But be assured we will fight all the way to the finish, 400 tricky miles away.*

This was very different sailing compared with conditions in the Southern Ocean. Maintaining a smooth watch system was crucial and having sufficient rest meant everyone would remain alert on deck.

Gordon:

You actually live on a leg like this. You eat the right food at the correct times. You only need to get up five minutes before you're required on deck, whereas in the Southern Ocean it's a 30-minute exercise to get dressed. The four-hours-on/four-hours-off watch system leaves you with 12 hours' sleeping time a day: quite a long time. When not wanting to sleep the guys on the off-watch will often wander around the deck, just relaxing, while the on-watch continues to sail the boat. This actually benefits the boat as it leads to a lot of continuity between the two watches — you go on watch fully aware of what has been happening in the last four hours. We had silky smooth watch changes as a result — there was no real break in the rhythm of the boat at any stage.

The *News Corp* team continued to cope extremely well under pressure they hadn't previously experienced. They realised that at some stage on every leg prior to this, except Leg One from Southampton to Cape Town, they had held the lead but hadn't been able to retain it. This time they were answering the challenge as the miles were being ticked off towards the Chesapeake.

Nick:

Day 4 — Twenty-five miles to the Chesapeake light. We have illbruck *1.5 miles behind and* Amer Sports One *a further half-mile back. They gain a little, then we gain a little, but the positions have been steady for a while now. There is a dogged determination onboard to do well. As I write, the other yachts are trying to climb up to windward of us: maybe they're looking for a little relief from an adverse current, or maybe they want to set themselves up in a different position for the 20-knot winds we're expecting. Maybe, though, they're just having their own little duel back there. Back to the radar to watch their progress.*

Team News Corp was recognised as the leader into Chesapeake Bay by being first to pass under the bridge at the 10-mile-wide entrance. Positions behind them had changed: there was only 1 mile to *Amer Sports One* and two to *illbruck*, while *ASSA ABLOY* was 18 miles astern. In last place, *djuice* was having another shocking run, 2 miles behind *Amer Sports Too* and 81 miles from the front. *SEB* wasn't doing much better — not that they weren't trying, as their new recruit, 2000 Olympic gold-medallist Mark Reynolds, explained: 'We started making sail changes, putting up different sails one after the other, sometimes only minutes apart. At first I thought the boys just wanted to show me all the nice sails they had, but after they had all been up once, we started going through them again.' Of course, once those sails came down, the crew had to repack them so they'd be ready to go again. It was hard work, especially moving them around the deck.

Jez declared that for the *News Corp* team Day 4 was going to be a tough one as they clawed their way through Chesapeake Bay: 'It's going to be a long, tense day in a dying breeze. Fifteen minutes ago *Amer Sports One* closed to within three boat-lengths of us as they caught the last of the old wind. A super-slick spinnaker change to our lightest sail has seen us open up the gap again to a quarter-mile. Last night it was a different story, as a snagged halyard during a sail change cost us the same distance. It's like a game of snakes and ladders, so let's hope the last roll of the dice gives us a ladder to finish on.'

With 100 miles to go, anything could happen in such changeable conditions. *illbruck* had gained a mile in the previous few hours, having fallen behind earlier that morning and the forecast was not for straightforward sailing. Jez described the crew as 'coiled springs ready to do whatever's needed to make a gain or save a boat length. I don't think I've ever been in a more intense yacht race.'

The tactical team onboard had decided that for maximum efficiency they should adopt an 'all hands on deck' strategy at the entrance to the bay. But after a couple of hours they realised that with the breeze dying it was going to take a lot longer to get to Baltimore than anticipated, so they returned to a normal watch system. 'It's always been a philosophy of mine to try to keep your powder dry in terms of making sure that people get a sleep,' Gordon said. 'It's very easy when you get into an area like Chesapeake Bay to imagine that the finish is just around the corner, when it's actually 120 miles away, a full 24 hours in these conditions. Also, when there are boats right alongside you, it's tempting to want to spend the whole time on deck to help make the boat go faster. But when it's this close, your mere presence can often be a distraction to the on-watch and not help the cause. It's more important that you put your head down and get some sleep.'

Gordon and Stuart Childerley were sharing the steering while Barney was the on-deck tactician, focusing on the weather patterns around the yacht, the location of the opposition and the positioning of *Team News Corp* on the course. He was working very closely with Matt Humphries, who was below deck watching the radar and depth sounder, and crunching all the navigation information that could be gleaned from the computer.

Jez's reference to snakes and ladders was proving to be the perfect analogy for the situation on the bay. With the sails hanging like limp clothes on a line, the *Team News Corp* crew could only watch while *Amer Sports One*'s spinnaker filled with a gentle puff — their rival began to close the gap. Within a few minutes they had drawn level with the still-motionless *Team News Corp. Amer Sports One* continued its glide ... into the lead. This was a real test for the *News Corp* team: they could not lose their nerve. There was nothing they could do about the situation. Their fight had just become that bit tougher — it was now a case of coming from behind. The situation called for full faith in the pre-race plan they'd established for the bay, especially considering the weather synopsis Nick was providing.

Barney:

> There is a well-known saying in this sport: 'Never sail towards a dying breeze.' We analysed the wind and

decided it was dying on the right-hand side of the bay. Thunderstorms were starting to develop over the land to the left, on the eastern side, so we expected a light offshore breeze to build on that side of the bay. Convinced we were right, we changed course and headed away from Amer Sports One. Much to our delight, after drifting along for only a short while, we found our breeze. Still, it was some of the weirdest sailing I've ever experienced. The surface of the bay was a mirror — there wasn't a breath of air. But at the mast top, 100 feet up, there was up to 12 knots of wind. To catch that breeze we had the spinnaker and mainsail set inside out — the tops were full and the bottoms were flapping. They looked ridiculous, but who cared, because we were coasting across a windless bay and leaving the others behind. We soon found ourselves four miles ahead of Amer. The only way they were going to catch us was if we 'parked'.

'It was a no-brainer,' Jez proclaimed, 'because we were actually heading towards the finish with the current helping us while the others weren't. It was a calculated gamble, but we had the weather reports saying we were doing the right thing.'

Annapolis, on Chesapeake Bay's eastern shore, is considered the nation's sailing capital, so naturally spectator boats converged on the fleet as they made their way slowly towards the finish line. There were also large crowds on the shore, most armed with binoculars, watching and commenting as *Team News Corp* established what looked to be a leg-winning lead. Still, the crew knew they had plenty of challenges ahead, none more so than the very narrow shipping channel they would have to negotiate during darkness. While reducing the opportunities of passing lanes for their pursuers, the narrowness of the channel also meant that it would be extremely dangerous trying to manoeuvre around any commercial shipping vessels during the night.

Within a few hours, their apprehension was borne out when confronted by two vessels at the narrowest part of the channel, a section just 200 metres wide.

Damian 'Shreda' Duke:

I looked back to see the lights of a tugboat coming towards us, so I called out to Matt and Gordon that it was approaching. When the tug was only a few hundred metres behind us I noticed it was towing an absolutely massive barge with a bluff bow. It was so wide it was taking up much of the channel, and the way it was coming at us left me in no doubt it was destined to overtake us where the channel was narrowest. There was virtually no breeze and we were doing only 4 knots upwind with the Code Zero set, so we had to keep our wits about us.

To make things worse, we needed to tack, and if we did so without the tug master knowing we were ahead of him, it could turn out to be quite nasty. I grabbed the VHF hand-held radio and called, 'Tugboat behind us, this is the yacht in front of you.' While I was talking to the tugboat captain, the captain of an outward-bound freighter came on the radio to say he was heading towards us from the opposite direction. I looked up the channel and, sure enough, there was a huge, 150-metre-long ship coming straight towards us. It was a case of, 'Bloody hell, we've really got a bit on here.'

The ship's captain was quite panicky, saying, 'I can't see you. I can see the tug, but I cannot see you.' It wasn't until the tug turned its spotlights on and lit us up that he could see us. I explained we were part of the Volvo race. The captain of the freighter took command of the situation, asking if it was possible for us to sail outside the channel. Matt, who was navigating, confirmed we could not go outside the channel because with 14 feet of keel under us, we would run aground.

I got back on the radio, explained we were leading the race and that we were not prepared to go outside the channel. The ship's captain came back and said, 'Well, I'm going to stick very close to the green markers this side.'

Then the tugboat's master said, 'And I'm going to stick very close to the red. We're going to have to work it out from there and see what we can do. This is going to be tough.'

There was constant conversation between the two captains and me as we tried to work out how to execute the pass. We could hardly manoeuvre the yacht because of the light wind, and they couldn't stop.

Of course, we were right in the middle of their passing point — we were going to be the meat in the sandwich. We lowered the Code Zero and set a jib to give us more manoeuvrability. Then, as they closed in on us, it became apparent that our only option was to position ourselves right in the centre of the channel so we would be between the ship and the barge. We decided that as they passed we would turn the yacht head to wind [slow the boat with sails flapping while it pointed into the wind]. There would be only boat-lengths to spare either side and we knew that if we didn't get the move right either the barge would plough right over the top of us or we'd crash into the side of the ship.

It worked. We missed the stern of the ship by just metres. We tacked over and steered towards Baltimore again. The ship's captain came back on the radio sounding pretty relieved. 'OK, I'm happy now that you're clear,' he said, and with that we all disappeared into the night. I put down the radio and realised I was shaking. It was incredibly close.

The Code Zero headsail went back up and *Team News Corp* continued on its way towards the finish. There was always the threat that the wind might die once more and trap them like a giant clam. Relief came for the crew when the city lights appeared after they rounded the final bend in the channel. They knew then that they were destined to be only the third yacht in the race so far to win a stage. It was just before 2am on 18 April, the fifth day of racing and Ross Field's birthday, when a small escort of media and support boats showed them the way to the line. The gun sounded and the crew went up as one. 'Yeeeessss!' was the shout. Handshakes, backslapping and high-fives followed. The grins had never been broader. Finally they had achieved what they always knew they could do. It had been a long time coming.

Their battle song, 'Stop the Rock', belted out across the harbour, letting much of a sleeping city know that the first yacht had finished. When *Team News Corp* emerged from the night to become illuminated by the city lights crewmembers could be seen dancing on deck while the crowd on the dock cheered, clapped and whistled. When the yacht was docked at the specially built floating pontoon, the team stepped ashore for the official welcome ceremony. Each crewmember was presented with a medallion, while Jez proudly held aloft the crystal trophy. Within seconds champagne was arcing through the air and drenching everyone standing too close. No one cared.

'It was a combination of things that won the leg,' Jez reported. 'Good boat, good sails, great crew, good planning, good preparation and a great sponsor. And we did have lady luck on our side occasionally. That's what yacht racing is all about: getting all those millions of little ingredients to come together.'

The sun was coming up when the celebrations ended and the crew headed for bed. They'd watched *Amer Sports One* pick up a new breeze and finish 26 minutes behind them, while *ASSA ABLOY* had made a remarkable recovery and nudged *illbruck* out of third place. The result saw *illbruck* remain a comfortable overall race leader on 41 points, followed by *ASSA ABLOY* on 34, *Amer Sports One* on 32, *Team News Corp* 31, *Tyco* 27, *Team SEB* 21, *djuice dragons* 20 and *Amer Sports Too* 10.

Top *Team News Corp* makes slow progress up Chesapeake Bay on its way to winning Leg Six.
Centre Skipper Jez Fanstone meets the media after arriving in Baltimore.
Bottom Savouring the moment, the *Team News Corp* crew enjoy their welcome in Baltimore.

All images *Richard Langdon/Ocean Images*

<< The fleet zig-zags its
way upwind on
Chesapeake Bay after
starting in Annapolis.
Rick Tomlinson

ANNAPOLIS
TO LA ROCHELLE

You must learn from the past, not live in it.

JEZ FANSTONE — SKIPPER, *TEAM NEWS CORP*

along with the exceptional popularity of the Volvo race among the locals, *Team News Corp*'s win on the leg from Miami meant that the crew were local legends during the stopover. Jez was hosted around town like a celebrity. One day he was seen wearing a huge stetson and cowboy boots (just to feel the part) while he presented trophies at a horse-race meeting; and one evening 20 000 people saw him deliver the opening pitch at a Baltimore Orioles baseball game — well, it was almost a pitch. It bounced over the plate.

The crew were also the centre of attention at the crowded trophy presentation party in the city centre; not that they were easy to recognise wearing their crew-issue navy-blue suits, blue shirts and dark-blue ties for the first time, a far cry from their regular sailing gear. They bounded onto the stage to enthusiastic applause and received the winner's trophy. Damian 'Shreda' Duke was named the recipient of the Seamanship Award for the leg following his efforts on the two-way radio when the yacht was in danger of being run down by the freighter and tug towing a barge. The captain of the freighter had commended Shreda for his radio manner and coolness in handling what was a very dangerous situation.

After a week in Baltimore the fleet took part in a Parade of Sail on Chesapeake Bay to the beautiful seaport village of Annapolis, where they would prepare for the start of the 3400-mile trans-Atlantic leg to La Rochelle, France, three days later. The crews were overwhelmed by the reception in Annapolis. Hundreds of boats escorted them into the city-front dock, where thousands of people waited to view the yachts and welcome the crews. Over the next three days they would sample the delights of one of the prettiest and oldest cities in America and taste the local seafood delicacies that have made Chesapeake Bay so famous.

Having come second and fourth on the two previous legs, the pressure was mounting on the outright race leader, John Kostecki and his *illbruck* team. *illbruck* had done well on all the long legs, so this stretch to La Rochelle would be their big chance to build on their points advantage. Kostecki opted to have Australian Noel Drennan join the crew in place of Ian Moore 'to provide additional helming and trimming skills'. He would also be their onboard sailmaker, which made him an important addition because on legs like this one the yachts normally experienced some sort of gear failure with the sails.

In terms of winning the race outright, *ASSA ABLOY* was looming as *illbruck*'s biggest threat, yet skipper Neal McDonald remained relaxed about his team's approach: 'All we have to do is push as hard as we can, be careful not to do anything silly and not take any terrible risks. Clearly, we will be very interested in where they [*illbruck*] are. If we see opportunities to take big jumps on them we might, but then again we don't want to lose the guys behind us.' What he was saying was that while wanting to beat *illbruck* they remained well aware that they had to keep the rest of the fleet well covered. Still, McDonald had decided to reinforce his crew by including Spain's Guillermo Altadill, a specialist offshore helmsman whose presence was considered to be even more valuable following the forecast for very strong winds.

Team News Corp was another boat to undergo an interesting crew change. Nick White stepped off to again become the yacht's shore-based meteorologist while Ross's 31-year-old son, Campbell, went aboard as navigator. Jez felt that Campbell, an electronics expert and respected navigator and yachtsman, would be an all-round asset, even when the going got tough on deck.

The course from Annapolis to La Rochelle, on the Bay of Biscay, would normally see the yachts sail the large arc of the great circle route which, because of the curvature of the earth, is the shortest track. The course is not a straight line between the ports. It would take them near the latitude of 50 degrees: Annapolis is at 39 degrees and La Rochelle 46 degrees. The major influences on this leg are the Gulf Stream and the chilly Labrador Current, plus the powerful storms often generated by low-pressure weather systems. The teams were in the middle of planning their weather and tactical strategies for the leg when the US Coast Guard and Canadian ice patrol services reported masses of icebergs between 43 degrees north, 50 degrees west and 45 degrees north, 45 degrees west. That put the 'bergs directly in the path the yachts would take, so the VOR Race Committee declared an 'ice box' — a no-go zone — for the leg. It was defined by the area 40N/58N, and 45W/51W. While it reduced the threat it still didn't guarantee the fleet would not be exposed to 'bergs (the *Titanic* sank after hitting an iceberg at around 40 degrees north exactly 90 years earlier in what was considered an average ice year).

The establishment of the no-go zone changed the entire complexion of the leg. It meant a far narrower racing lane, making the leg more of a procession, thereby eliminating many of the tactical ploys that would otherwise be available to the crews. It would now be easier for *illbruck* to keep the opposition covered.

Miserable was the only way to describe the weather on 28 April 2002, the start of the seventh stage of the race. It was cold and windy with heavy rain belting down from grey clouds charging across the sky like raging surf. Still, thousands of people gathered around the dock to cheer the teams on as they departed for the start area underneath the Bay Bridge. Out on the water the abysmal weather hadn't deterred hundreds of spectator boats from assembling for the farewell, from small dinghies being tossed around on the choppy waters to large commercial charter vessels.

As low cloud shrouded the bridge and driving rain hindered visibility the eight yachts, with full mainsails and their second largest jibs set, charged away from the start line, then passed under the bridge before targeting the mouth of Chesapeake Bay and the Atlantic Ocean 140 miles away. Not only did they have to negotiate their way through the enthusiastic spectator fleet, they were confronted with an adverse tidal flow, shallows and crab pots that could snag on their keels. And hanging over the crews was a weather forecast for cold and rough conditions on the Atlantic, with northwesterly winds gusting to 30 knots. There was little to look forward to, except possibly if you were aboard *illbruck*: the wind angle would make it an across-the-wind reach to the first corner of the ice exclusion zone. For them it was like being able to turn on a turbo-charger — the conditions could not have been more ideal for the yacht that had already proven virtually unbeatable when hard reaching.

Sure enough, with little more than 24 hours of the race behind them, *illbruck* was setting the pace two miles ahead of *ASSA ABLOY* with another two miles to *Team News Corp* and *Tyco*. As the fleet sailed deeper into the depression bringing the rough weather, average speeds increased in proportion to the rising wind strength. In one six-hour period the averages climbed from 10 knots to 18 knots. The yachts were also experiencing the Gulf Stream, which was acting like a giant slingshot on their ride towards Europe. Research by team meteorologists revealed that the stream moves up to 150 million cubic metres of water per second and travels at 5 knots at its strongest point of flow!

The minor places behind *illbruck* were changing at regular intervals. *Team News Corp*, which reported two near-collisions with whales, had moved into second spot, 9 miles in arrears, with *Team SEB* close at hand. *ASSA ABLOY* moved back to fourth. As the wind strength grew, the sailmakers in each crew became increasingly anxious and began experiencing bouts of insomnia.

Alby Pratt — sailmaker/trimmer, *Team News Corp*

It has been a bit of a rude awakening to be back in the heavy running conditions after the easy going of the last two legs. Being the onboard sailmaker means you are never at ease when the wind is starting to blow from behind and the heavier spinnakers go up. You are always on edge, thinking that at any minute the sail is going to explode and sentence you to a 12-hour stint of solitary confinement down below, sitting in the bilge hunched over the sewing machine, putting it all back together. Being off watch isn't any better. You sleep with one eye on the wind speed readout, which is mounted on the forward bulkhead, always saying silent prayers that the breeze isn't going to increase the extra knot that will put the sail into the red zone.

The average speeds just kept rising and rising. As *illbruck* continued to expand their lead John Kostecki reported that the northwesterly wind was providing them with ideal reaching conditions for maintaining top speed. With the assistance of 2 to 3 knots of current they averaged over 20 knots for the last 12 hours on Day 2. In those conditions it was incredibly wet on deck — Kostecki likened it to a constant fire-hose spray. The one consolation was that the water was very warm — around 24 degrees Celsius.

illbruck's average speed kept growing higher and soon it became apparent that big news was coming. *ILLBRUCK* BREAKS WORLD RECORD was the headline trumpeted by the VOR race office on Day 3. The German yacht had covered 473 nautical miles (average speed 19.708 knots) in 24 hours, erasing the previous record of 467.7 nautical miles held by Frenchman Bernard Stamm's Open 60-class yacht, *Amor Lux*. The news didn't stop the *illbruck* team from pushing even harder and a few hours later they had lifted the mark to a staggering 484 miles.

John Kostecki — skipper, *illbruck*

When we saw that we had a 127-mile run in six hours we started to do the maths and realised we had a good shot at breaking the record. We didn't try to [do it] . . . it just happened. Our goal is to win a podium finish on this leg, so we're fully focused on that, not breaking records. We broke the record by pushing the boat hard in favourable conditions — we managed to play the Gulf Stream well, slightly better than our competitors, which added to our overall boat speed.

As the eight yachts continued thundering across the Atlantic towards the southern limit of the no-go zone (which would end close to the midway point of their passage), *Tyco* reported a 470-mile day, *ASSA ABLOY* 471 miles and *Team SEB* 468. The one surprise was that *Team News Corp* had cascaded down the positions board to be fifth, 38 miles off the lead, trailing *illbruck*, *ASSA ABLOY*, *Tyco* and *Team SEB*. The only clue as to what might have contributed to their demise came in a report from Jez: 'We hit something just as the sun was coming up today — it must have been a shark or a sunfish. We must have had something caught because the boat slowed right down. It was still too dark to see what was going on, but we pulled the spinnaker down to stop the boat and free the obstruction.

Once it got light we could see through the endoscope [a through-hull looking glass] that paint had been scraped off the rudder. Something must have a headache today.'

The problem turned out to be a huge headache for the *Team News Corp* crew. Within 48 hours it was obvious something was wrong with the boat. Progress was slow, and despite a series of sail changes and re-trimming of the boat, there was no improvement in speed.

On Day 6 when they couldn't hold *Amer Sports One* in the same conditions they had been able to before — light winds with a Code Zero set — they knew something was up. Checking the keel and rudder constantly, when they could see the entire rudder, they confirmed that the tip of the foil had been knocked off. '[We] decided we wouldn't make our problem common knowledge to the fleet,' Jez reported later, 'because it might have influenced their tactics towards us at a later stage of the leg. If they knew we were wounded they might not give us an opportunity to try for a passing lane.'

While again bringing up the rear, the *Amer Sports Too* team reported they too were trying their hardest: 'It's wet and wild out here,' said skipper Lisa McDonald. 'This is the kind of sailing these boats like, fully powered up and reaching/surfing down the waves. Everyone is getting tired and I hope with every sail change that it is the right one. The sky is very grey with heavy low cloud and a few storm-like features looming about on the horizon. Best not to get tangled up with them.'

A few hours later the news from McDonald wasn't good. Hearing a loud 'bang', the crew witnessed all but the lower 10 metres of the carbon fibre mast crashing over the side when a rigging attachment failed. Their race was run. After ensuring no one was injured the 13 crewmembers set about getting the broken section and the sails back on deck. Once things were secure and a jury rig established using the stump of the mast and storm sails, they considered their options: 2500 miles eastwards to France or 400 miles northwest to Halifax in Nova Scotia. With the latter the obvious choice, they announced their retirement from the leg. As the yacht limped towards its destination the shore crew looked into finding a cargo ship that could freight the yacht to Europe, where it would be re-rigged and, with a bit of luck, readied in time for the start of the penultimate leg of the race on 25 May; just over three weeks away.

Neal McDonald (Lisa's husband) — skipper, *ASSA ABLOY*

Poor Lisa and her team on Amer Sports Too: *after man overboard or fire, losing a mast is about the worst thing to happen at sea. I hear the crew is unharmed which is the most important thing — but what do they do next? I hope they make land reasonably quickly and get organised for France. I can't imagine the disappointment and worry. I hope it all works out OK for them. Compared to what they have had to deal with, ASSA ABLOY has had it easy.*

BY DAY 6 the wind was abating and the seven remaining racers slowed as they sailed east along the southern perimeter of the ice box. Apart from *illbruck*, fleet positions continued to be shaky. 'Yesterday and this morning saw us making good gains on the fleet and moving into second place,' reported *Tyco*'s Kevin Shoebridge. 'This all changed later this morning when the strong reaching conditions stopped and we flopped around for a few hours in 9 knots of wind. *ASSA ABLOY* has taken second spot and we are losing to *News Corp* and *SEB* in the south.'

The fleet's speed across the Atlantic was still quite remarkable, however, and it wouldn't be long before the wind was back to make their progress even more impressive. On Day 6 *illbruck* turned the corner of the ice box and aimed northeast towards La Rochelle, 1929 miles away. Kostecki's team held a 19-mile lead over *ASSA ABLOY* and 28 miles over *Tyco*.

Jez reported from *Team News Corp*: 'Good speed now and making gains on the two boats around us [*SEB* and *Amer Sports One*] as the breeze builds. Getting ready for 40 knots running. The boat is finally dried out but shortly we will be submariners again!' It all sounded very positive; part of their ongoing desire not to let the opposition know about their rudder problems.

And blow it did — with almost dire consequences for *Team SEB*. With gusts of up to 43 knots a gigantic wave submerged the whole boat, washing trimmer Glen Kessels away from a coffee grinder winch pedestal towards the stern. Miraculously, he was able to hang on and stop himself from being washed overboard. 'Now we have only half the steering wheel on the port side,' skipper Gurra Krantz said when he reported in. 'Glen's body knocked the other half off when he went cockpit surfing ... [it] looks like one of those airplane steering wheels that is only half a circle.'

Not even the navigators, perched below deck in their claustrophobic little cubicles under the cockpit, were spared in these conditions.

Mark Rudiger — navigator, *ASSA ABLOY*

Almost 22-knot average boat speed lately ... a wild fire hose reach [fast, furious and very wet sailing across the wind]! I'm constantly keeping the guys updated on deck through my little hatch in the nav. station. I'm yelling at the top of my voice to be heard over the wind and boat noise: 'First wave of [weather] front passing now, next wave two to three hours. Could be up to 38 knots like the last one. Watch for steep waves. Course over ground right on the money. We gained 1 mile on illbruck, *and 6 degrees bearing and 1 mile on* Tyco. *Keep the pedal down!'*

I quickly close the hatch as another ton of water gushes down the cockpit. Everyone is perched way back on the stern with main and spinnaker sheet in hand. The grinder runs forward once in a while to grind. Everything in the boat is stacked aft. Whoaaaaah! Big wind and the boat begins to broach. I'm fully spreadeagled and braced in the nav. station. The sails flog, the boat shudders and quickly shakes it off as we tear off down another wave. You're going to have a few of those if you're pushing the edge. After 48 hours of these conditions the nerves are getting a little frayed, and the commands are getting a little tenser at times. Fun is fast! Stay loose. Work together. Looks like some bumps in the road ahead. May have to check the seat belts and get the crash helmets ready.

With just over 1000 miles to go before savouring escargot and French wine, the procession continued in an orderly fashion: *illbruck, ASSA ABLOY, Tyco, SEB, Team News Corp, Amer Sports One* and *djuice*...until *SEB*'s Gurra Krantz decided that the only way to climb out of fourth and make an impression on the lead was to change course dramatically — to the south. It was a nerve-wracking time as Gurra and the crew waited to see whether their move from the pack was going to pay off. Gurra reported that they did expect losses to begin with, but hoped for gains over the next 24 hours. They had their fingers crossed.

Others weren't so sure *Team SEB* had got it right.

Dee Smith — navigator, *Amer Sports One*

Day 8 — This has been a wildly fast race so far. The three leaders have done such a good job in getting their hard-earned leads. But it can turn inside out in the next 36 hours. In front of the fleet a ridge is building and everyone has to pass it. All bets are off as to who will win this leg. SEB has taken the southern route for the last day. It was an early split from the fleet and might pay off big. Only problem is they will have to sail upwind to the finish, and that angle might make them pay. illbruck, on the other hand, has protected their lead to the north and has sailed up in front of Tyco and ASSA ABLOY. News Corp, djuice and Amer Sports One are in the middle. We are within 10 miles of each other and are hoping our little pack can pass the leading three, and that SEB's route is just wrong. We are only about three hours behind the leaders at this speed. If they stop ahead of us then it is a complete restart. Luck could play a big part in the finish.

Besides world-champion yachtsman Stuart Childerley, who was enjoying the challenge and exhilaration of his first Atlantic crossing, the *Team News Corp* crew weren't having the best of times on the race course after encountering an extremely unfavourable wind shift.

Jez:
> *Had a bad afternoon yesterday when the wind went light and we were forced onto a course which, for more than an hour, had us pointing more towards Pom Rock [UK] than France. Amer Sports One is now 11 miles ahead, but Bluey is giving her all in these last hours of the leg. We've taken 5 miles out of Amer One in three hours.*

This was a remarkable effort, considering the additional drag that was being generated by the damaged rudder.

The *illbruck* crew were feeling far more comfortable with their position on the course but, unfortunately, far less comfortable healthwise. A serious stomach virus had brought down five crewmembers, making them bilious and barely able to operate. Luckily they were feeling better when the pressure of the closing stages of the leg began to build. They could sense the blocking high-pressure ridge developing around them as the wind faded to a faint breeze. It was a hurdle they had to be well clear of before the competition if they were to be first to La Rochelle.

Richard Clarke — helmsman/trimmer, *illbruck*
> *Practically licked the leeward bilge dry to make sure we're carrying no excess weight, especially to leeward.*
>
> *What a difference a day makes ... no more blast reaching. Thought we were starting to grow gills with so much water over the deck. Now we're plodding along with a Code Zero up, dry tops off, one guy driving, one*

trimming the traveller, and three guys chilling. Got a bit dicey a few hours ago. Thought we were going to be swallowed up by the ridge and left drifting in no wind. We had only 1.5 knots of boat speed and tensions were high as we wondered how the rest of the fleet was faring. You could have heard the huge sigh of relief echoing across the Atlantic after the last sked came in ... no big losses. Still looks like a few more obstacles to overcome, but with the ridge hopefully behind us we will all feel a bit lighter.

It wasn't long before the *illbruck* crew were able to lighten up. After little more than 10 days at sea, and with 100 miles to go until the ancient towers marking La Rochelle's harbour entrance came into view, the German entry was holding a very comfortable 40-mile lead over *ASSA ABLOY*. This was the point on the lap around the planet where the fleet crossed their outbound track, so in essence they had completed their circumnavigation.

Team SEB's 'no guts, no glory' attack on the leaders by changing course to the south didn't work and came close to costing them a valuable fourth place. They crossed the finish line behind *illbruck*, *ASSA ABLOY*, and *Tyco* and just 10 minutes ahead of *Amer Sports One*.

Team News Corp couldn't match the pace of the others over the last few days and arrived an extremely disappointing sixth. As soon as Bluey crossed the line a crewman went over the side to check the rudder. He surfaced to confirm that 45 centimetres (18 inches) of the tip of the foil had been broken off.

Gordon Maguire:
When we were sailing downwind and in light airs the problem with the rudder wasn't a huge handicap, but it really affected our performance during the last week, sailing into La Rochelle, when we did a lot of two-sail reaching. When reaching the boat heels over a lot, which means that the shape of the boat sailing through the

water changes; it always wants to turn up into the wind, so you have to use a lot more rudder to keep the boat going straight. If the rudder is smaller than it's supposed to be you have to use more rudder than you would normally to keep the boat on course. When you do that you are applying a brake to the boat. It's increased drag. The design of these rudders is very sophisticated, not unlike the wings of aeroplanes which have tips designed to minimise drag vortices. When the tip of the rudder is missing you have a mass of vortices coming off the bottom of the blade creating even more drag. We were basically dragging our heels all the way to La Rochelle.

I calculated after the finish that we would have had to sail 1.5 per cent faster to beat illbruck. It's very difficult to put an actual figure on what the rudder damage cost us, but I consider it could have affected our speed by up to 3 per cent.

The *Team News Corp* crew were adamant that they weren't making excuses. A broken rudder is a fact of life in sailing, just like a blown tyre wrecks the day for a race-car driver. This was merely another frustration with a boat that kept showing the potential to be out in front, but more often than not just couldn't deliver. 'You must learn from the past, not live in it,' said a philosophical Jez. 'There's no point looking back. We could have been sitting here in La Rochelle in third place overall and still have a shot at second place. But we're not, so we just have to get on with it and do the best we can on the two remaining legs.'

≪ Thank you and goodbye.
The *ASSA ABLOY* crew salutes
La Rochelle as they leave for
the dash to Gothenburg.
Rick Tomlinson

≫ LA ROCHELLE TO GOTHENBURG

The boat is literally sending itself on a suicide mission.

EMMA WESTMACOTT — WATCH LEADER, *AMER SPORTS TOO*

La Rochelle was a wonderful entrée to Europe for the VOR racers and their supporters. The narrow and winding cobblestone streets of this medieval port and village are like canyons, carving their way through tiny terraced streetfront residences and shops. Cosy restaurants offered the sailors a mouthwatering array of fresh seafood.

Unfortunately, though, the crew of *Amer Sports Too* had little time to appreciate the ambience of this beautiful city. They had done a remarkable job even to be there in time for the start of Leg Eight. After sailing the dismasted and jury-rigged yacht to Halifax in Nova Scotia, with the help of their shore team they arranged for it to be shipped to England to be re-rigged before heading to La Rochelle. It was a mammoth effort — first the yacht travelled in the cargo hold of a freighter to Liverpool, where it was loaded onto the deck of a small coastal ship and transported to Southampton. There, it was unloaded and motored to Gosport, near Portsmouth, for the new mast to be fitted. The crew then sailed it across to La Rochelle, where they arrived with less than a week to spare before the restart. 'I wasn't really sure that we'd make it but I've been brought up with the philosophy that where there is a will there is a way; the only way you will get forward is by looking forward,' said a relieved Lisa McDonald.

If there was a spotlight shining on these two remaining stages, it was firmly focused on two of the race's disappointments so far, *djuice dragons* and *Team SEB*, both of which were entering home territory. *djuice*'s Knut Frostad, who had gone into the VOR amid considerable fanfare, was copping a pasting in the media and from the public in his native Norway. He announced some drastic crew changes for Leg Eight, bringing Kiwi Erle Williams on and dropping two, including navigator Jean-Yves Bernot. *SEB*'s Gurra Krantz, from Sweden, had promised so much for this race, having finished third in 1997/98. But he had not yet been able to deliver this time around. Both teams were hoping for a good performance on the upcoming leg to ease the pressure coming from outside.

The surprise for the *Team News Corp* camp was that three of their former crewmates were back in the race — the lure had been too great. Jeff Scott had also joined *djuice*, while Jon Gunderson and Steve Cotton were aboard *SEB*. There was one change on their own boat, with

Stuart Childerley answering the call of business back in England. Fellow Englishman and world champion of sailing Jeremy Robinson replaced him as a back-up helmsman. 'We're ready to go,' said Jez. 'We've put a new rudder in, re-cut some sails and got in some new ones. Our real race now is for third place overall, but there's still an outside chance we can get second. This is a leg that you can divide into five parts and there's no denying it will be tough. The only thing we don't like is the stretch they've put us on along the coast of Norway, where we have to sail around masses of rocks. It's dangerous . . .'

La Rochelle sits midway along the coast of the Bay of Biscay, a stretch of water with a horrible reputation for wild weather, and two days before the start it looked like a storm was already aiming right at the VOR fleet. Conditions were going to be rugged for at least the first 24 hours of the 1075-mile stretch north to Sweden and the finish line at Gothenburg. Considered a sprint, the leg was as much an obstacle course as a test of sailing. There were 30 points on the course that needed to be negotiated — a navigator's nightmare. The obstacles started with the massive spring tides that cause powerful and swirling currents along the coasts of France and England. Then there was the English Channel, which to shipping is the equivalent of a Los Angeles freeway in rush hour; and after that, the North Sea with its hundreds of oil rigs that stand like tenpins. As if those man-made hurdles would not be enough of a test, there were the natural hazards — drying sandbanks and shoals. Further along the course a minefield of islands, rocks and reefs would ensure there would be no free ride along the coast of Norway, which had to be skirted en route to Gothenburg.

There was still plenty of excitement and drama to be played out in the race. Outright leader *illbruck* was still beatable, but could wrap up first place with a good result on this leg. *ASSA ABLOY*, which was sailing to its home port, remained *illbruck*'s arch-rival, and skipper Neal McDonald wanted to keep it that way on what was a crucial leg. Just to make sure they could have every chance of winning he arranged for Swedish crewmember Klas 'Klabbe' Nylof to travel to Norway during the stopover to study the coastal navigational hazards they would face.

Even more open was the fight for third overall, with only eight points separating *ASSA ABLOY* in second place and *Tyco* in fifth. *Amer Sports One* was third and *Team News Corp* fourth.

The flags flapping frenetically around the old port in La Rochelle on the afternoon of 25 May 2002, the start day of Leg Eight, confirmed that the gale warnings issued had been no false alarm. Crews were far from enthusiastic about what was coming their way — total punishment: upwind sailing in heinous conditions for the first 180 miles to Ushant, an island off France's northwest coast and the point at which they would turn the corner and head north to the English Channel. 'It's about boat speed, but it's also about holding the boat together,' said Jez as *Team News Corp* was about to depart the dock for the start. 'Forty-knot winds are a great equaliser and regardless of how good your boat is, if it's not in one piece, you won't be going anywhere.'

The eight yachts began their colourful parade out of the harbour before thousands of well-wishers. While the sailors weren't looking forward to the first stage of the leg, the rough weather certainly hadn't dampened the enthusiasm of the locals. There were hundreds of spectator craft, even some hardy souls on windsurfers and jet skis, and two tall ships, which were docked as though forming a guard of honour for the fleet and crowded with colourfully dressed supporters. As each yacht motored past the towers at the harbour entrance, fireworks exploded overhead.

The *ASSA ABLOY* team, who needed to stamp their authority on this leg from the start, appeared destined to do that with a perfectly timed run towards the leeward end of the start line, just as the gun was about to fire. But then … disaster! The huge, yellow inflated buoy indicating the outer limit of the start line was chasing *ASSA ABLOY* — and catching up. The anchor line on the buoy was too long and the excess line had hooked itself on either the keel or the rudder. Neal McDonald, trying to keep his cool, had no option but to slow the yacht and dispose of their unwanted appendage. Shedding his foul-weather gear, bowman Jason Carrington jumped into the bitterly cold water and swam to the rudder. He dived down and soon realised the line was caught on the keel. To save time another crewmember, Richard Mason, jumped in and, armed with a knife, swam to the buoy to cut the line. The two crew were hauled back aboard and then, with the buoy gone and the situation under control, McDonald slammed the yacht through a 360-degree turn, the penalty they had to pay under race rules for 'hitting the mark or any part of it'.

When *ASSA ABLOY* resumed racing the leaders were on a power reach in the stiff breeze and more than eight minutes ahead. *Team News Corp*, boasting a double head rig — jib and staysail — was the leader, two boat-lengths in front of *illbruck*, with *Amer Sports One* close behind. As they reached the mark the crews hauled in the sails and trimmed the boats to sail upwind — into hell, a crashing, bashing, smashing and horrendous haul upwind. Unfortunately Lisa McDonald and her team didn't get the smooth exit they'd hoped for when they came to the mark — badly misjudging the rounding, they hit the buoy and were forced to go around again.

After a few short tacks the fleet lined up for the push to Ushant, with *Amer Sports One* gaining from a windshift and taking the lead from *illbruck* and *Team News Corp*, who were just about side by side. By then the wind was coming out of the southwest at 25 knots and building, so the yachts faced a straight-line port tack slog all the way to Ushant, 180 miles away. There would be no passing lanes, just a demand for the highest possible speed in atrocious conditions. A counter-current soon had the steep seas cresting at 20 feet, making each wave a body-jarring experience. The yachts were spearing off the peaks into midair and crashing into the troughs — it was like the impact associated with smashing a truck into a brick wall every 15 or so seconds. 'These waves are very hard to predict and take you by surprise,' Lisa McDonald reported. 'It's a bit like hearing a car come to a screeching halt; you pause and cringe for a moment to hear if there is a crash. There's either a big sigh of relief when there's no noise or the shock/horror of an incident.'

With the yachts being hurled through the air and crashing around incessantly, one below-deck task required of the crew at the start of each leg became extremely difficult to execute this time. Within six hours of the start they had to attach a seal supplied by race officials to the propeller shaft and photograph it in place. That photograph, which shows the number on the seal, is then transmitted to the race office to confirm that the shaft has been sealed. This seal ensures that the yacht's propeller is not engaged when the crews run the engine for battery charging — a race official goes aboard each yacht at the end of the leg to cross-check the seal number on the shaft.

illbruck mastman Jamie Gale claimed the first night out to be the roughest of the race, even worse than the time the yacht almost sank south of Cape Town. *Amer Sports Too*'s watch leader, Emma Westmacott, said this initial part of the leg was something she'd rather forget: 'The boat is literally sending itself on a suicide mission, coming off the tops of the waves and thundering down into the crevasse beneath with an almighty shudder. On deck yet another chick is hanging over the side wishing she were anywhere but here, getting beaten up and shaken around like a martini. We had seven out of 13 chicks being sick, a big toll on the energy front. Having half the crew down is a disaster. And the other half are exhausted covering for them.'

Seasickness was pervading the fleet. 'Very unpleasant conditions have resulted in some of the crew spending time on the white telephone to God,' was the message from *Team News Corp*'s Matt Humphries as the yacht battled howling head winds of up to 45 knots. And from *djuice* came a report from helmsman/trimmer Stig Westergaard that some of the most experienced sailors onboard had been hit hard.

The fleet passed Ushant, a spectacular rocky outcrop carved into bold shapes by storms over millions of years, with little time to take in the bleak beauty of the region — they were achieving remarkable speeds after turning the corner. The sails were eased and spinnakers set, *Tyco* being the fastest at 20.4 knots in 35 knots of wind. Grant Dalton's *Amer Sports One* had sailed impressively to hold a narrow lead, but *illbruck*, *Tyco*, *SEB*, *News Corp* and *ASSA ABLOY* were all within three miles. *ASSA ABLOY* made a big inroad into the leading pack by staying closer to the French coast in better wind and less current after rounding the lighthouse off Ushant, while the others headed further towards the coast of England, with Dover Strait their target.

No crew was going to lie down on this leg; the racing became closer and closer, so much so that there were often times where no one could actually claim the lead. The top six (excluding *djuice* and *Amer Sports Too*) were sometimes line abreast, all determined to keep the competition in sight. And as the wind followed the forecast and became lighter, so the intensity of the racing mounted. The progress of the fleet was made even more difficult by the desire to sail as closely as possible to the English coast to avoid the strong adverse tidal flow.

'We're in the same wind as the two boats [*Tyco* and *ASSA ABLOY*] ahead of us, and that's important,' was the word on Day 3 from a satisfied Jez aboard *Team News Corp*. 'It's a bit tricky out here with the tides, and there'll be quite a few gybes as we continue around the English coast. There'll be a few more gains and losses, but we're looking good for the next stretch from England to Norway.' There was time for some contemplation among the crew, especially with the coast of England in sight. Shreda was twitching, looking longingly towards the Isle of Wight 55 miles away, where he knew his mates would be gathered in the Pier View Hotel in Cowes enjoying a pint. It was hard for him to believe that in just over two weeks this nine-month-long race would be over and he'd be back there with them, enjoying his own pint, telling tales of the VOR and planning his next adventure.

The sailing slug-fest continued unabated — news from the navigator of a gain of two boat-lengths on an opponent in the past 20 minutes brought jubilation. But there were no guarantees that the gain could be maintained, especially when unforeseen obstacles came into play. That was the case for *Team News Corp* when they reached Dover, one of the busiest ports for trans-Channel ferries.

Gordon Maguire:

> It was night and we were sailing just metres off the seawall at Dover, so close in fact that we couldn't see over the top of the wall and into the harbour. We'd spent 24 hours getting past Amer Sports One and at that stage had a lead of 10 boat-lengths on them. As we came to the harbour entrance a ferry appeared from behind the wall two boat-lengths in front of us and charged across our bow. It just filled the sky. We had no clue it was coming. All we could do was alter course towards the seawall and hope we'd get behind it. We missed the back of the thing by less than a boat-length, but with all the turbulence it created we just stopped. Suddenly everything we'd gained in the past day was lost. Amer was right back with us.

Leaving Dover Strait on Day 3 and sailing into the North Sea was like going through a gate and entering a paddock. Suddenly there was space for the fleet to play in, if not for the impediments presented by the hundreds of oil platforms and the shallows.

Ed Adams — tactician, *illbruck*

Yesterday the fleet lined up for a parade beneath the White Cliffs of Dover (yes, they are just as striking in real life as in the photos), passing within a boat-length of the breakwater to avoid the foul tide. From there it was a tricky series of gybes to snake inside the shoals that run up the English coast. Again, the yachts all had the same tide books, the same wind models, and followed the same path. After crossing the Thames Estuary, the fleet struck out for the M1 oil platform [a mark of the course]. At one point we crossed one of the many shoals (the North Sea is quite shallow) with only five feet of water under the keel, a strange feeling when you are out of sight of land. The seascape is littered with huge oil platforms, making it look like a set from a Star Wars *battlefield.*

The fleet had reached the halfway mark of Leg Eight and it was the closest racing so far — just one mile separating six boats, *Tyco*, *ASSA ABLOY*, *Team News Corp*, *SEB*, *Amer Sports One* and *illbruck*. Now that there was plenty of sea room the crews had the opportunity to make a tactical move. But would anyone be game? *SEB*'s Gurra Krantz was. He decided the time was right to put a schism between his boat and the rest of the pack, even though he was right there at the front. He chose a course change that would take *SEB* to a parallel track 10 miles to the northwest of the others, a gambit he thought might bring better wind and, as a consequence, more speed. It was a disastrous move. In a matter of hours *SEB* lost 10 miles on the five others and went back to sixth.

All boats were now experiencing big problems with massive clumps of kelp wrapping around keels and rudders, causing significant speed loss. 'Backing down', a technique where only the mainsail is left set while the yacht is sailed backwards to wash off the offending kelp, was becoming a finely executed manoeuvre, but it wasn't always successful — as *djuice dragons*' Stig Westergaard explained: 'We lost a bit of distance last night when we had to send poor Nocka [Anthony Nossiter] down for a refreshing, as he calls it, swim to clear some serious seaweed off the foils [keel and rudder]. It was pitch dark with just a faint moon giving him a hint of light to work with. Dressed only in a swimming costume, the big fellow took it on as few would have. The water was obviously very cold … when he got out and was observed I'd say it was about two centimetres' worth.'

When it came to fouled foils on this leg the prize for the best story went to *ASSA ABLOY*.

Mark Rudiger — navigator, *ASSA ABLOY*

All of a sudden we slowed down noticeably and the fleet was all over us. We checked the foils, and could see something on the keel. Nelly [Neal McDonald] pulled off a full head-to-wind backdown perfectly and in minutes we were bearing away again and putting the spinnaker back up. Magnus [Olsson] came up on deck, shaking his head, and exclaimed in his drawn-out Swedish accent, 'You won't believe what was on the keel — three big fishes.' He laughed, spreading his arms as far as he could to reveal the size. We were all suspicious of another Magnus Olsson fish story, but Richard [Clarke] and Sidney [Gavignet] confirmed the story, having watched through the [hull] scope.

Ask any crew and they'd say that the unsung heroes in this race are the sailors on the foredeck. With just one more leg to go it was the appropriate time to recognise these vital cogs in the racing mechanism.

Mikael Lundh — bowman, *djuice dragons*

Today is the day to write this tribute! There are many heroes in this race, from shore crew to sailing crew, but there are only 16 bowmen and women and they are the real beasts when it comes to being wet, cold and at altitude onboard these racing machines. They sacrifice themselves for the cause of hoisting and taking down sails in any weather, storm or gale; it really doesn't matter, they just do it. Very often they come down from the [spinnaker] pole or the mast with a big smile on their face knowing that they'd just done another awesome manoeuvre or saved the boat from a major disaster. They don't question their orders, they simply carry them out … SERVE AND PROTECT! … words whispered by bowmen around the world.

Later on Day 4 the intensity of the battle for the front five continued northwest across the North Sea to Norway, with its heavily pockmarked coastline. There was still no indication as to which yacht would win the leg, and a new game was coming into play — short tacking every few minutes until reaching Torunger Lighthouse, 1.5 miles off the Norwegian coast, where they would do a tight turn and head to Gothenburg. This would involve over 50 tacks.

Team News Corp watch leader Barney Walker told of a tough time sailing along the Norwegian coast: 'A cold front came through and we had a fantastic beat upwind with the four other leading boats. It was blowing about 28 knots and we were tacking every 10 minutes. It was one of the toughest times in this entire race. If you didn't stay close to the shore you lost ground, so we all had to keep digging deep for maximum effort. We made a mistake early when we moved all the equipment to windward every time we tacked. We soon figured out that it was costing us time and tiring us out so we ended up just stacking everything in the middle and concentrating on sailing the boat fast. It was just fantastic racing, with the entire crew on deck for 12 hours. Normally when you have a good yacht race, it's with one or two boats. Here there were five, all crewed by the best sailors in the world. It was an unforgettable experience.'

More than 40 spectator boats packed with enthusiastic race supporters had ventured out from Norway to watch the early-morning rounding of Torunger Island on Day 5, and they weren't disappointed. *ASSA ABLOY* was first around at 0836, followed by *illbruck* at 0846; *Tyco* 0848; *Team News Corp* 0852; *Amer Sports One* 0859; and *Team SEB* 0934.

Mark Rudiger — navigator, *ASSA ABLOY*

> *You could cut the tension with a knife. Magnus [watch leader] is running around like a cat on a hot tin roof trying to make up his mind about which way to go. Yesterday, when SEB was ahead for a little while, we had to sedate him and lash him in his bunk. Klabbe [Klas Nylof, trimmer] is keeping his cool, but his eyes show an intensity that is a sure sign of an explosion waiting to go off. The rest of us aren't much better after doing about 55 tacks up the Norwegian coast that left a track on the GPS plotter that looks more like a saw blade.*

Meanwhile, the *Team News Corp* crew were starting to think they had a fatal attraction for large ships ...

Gordon Maguire:

> *We were on the final 100 miles to the finish and well positioned a boat-length in front of* illbruck *and about four boat-lengths in front of* Amer Sports One. *It was a nice position to hold, sandwiched in the middle with our nose in front and heading to Sweden. We were sailing along in about 6 knots of breeze, doing nearly 7 knots of boat speed, when we noticed a huge, high-speed car-carrying ferry heading for us on an apparent collision course at 20 knots from abeam. We didn't want to compromise our position with the other two boats so we held our course, all the while hoping this massive ship charging at us would change course just a few degrees and go behind us. Barney was reporting on the ship's progress, saying, 'Oh, we don't have an issue ... we don't have an issue ... OK, we might have a little issue.'*

*I was steering and looked across at the ship. All I could
say was, 'Barney, this is a big issue. This thing is doing 20
knots and it's going to mow us down.' All the ship's master
needed to do was alter course 5 degrees and he would
have missed the whole fleet, but instead he wanted to
drive right through the middle of us, which he did. It was
inevitable that if he didn't change course we would smash
into the side of the ship as it went past. At the same time
we had to hold our course for as long as possible to keep
the other boats covered. The ship continued coming so at
the last moment I swerved the yacht and missed its stern
by a boat-length. There was terrible wind and water
turbulence in its wake so we initially lost ground to the
others, but because it was going directly upwind and we
were so close we got back into clear wind and water
sooner than* Amer Sports One *and* illbruck.

It was late on the evening of the fourth day at sea when spectator boats from ports all along the Swedish coast started converging on the yachts as the most incredible finish in the history of the event began to unfold. Neal McDonald and the *ASSA ABLOY* team were under incessant pressure as they desperately tried to retain their lead and keep alive their hopes of winning the race outright. An unfavourable change in wind direction saw them heading for the rocks and the only way to minimise their loss was to sail to a point where they were within metres of running aground, then tack. This they did and while their advantage had been chopped to pieces they were still in front — just. Only one mile separated the first five yachts — *ASSA ABLOY, illbruck, Tyco, News Corp* and *Amer Sports One*. 'The best racing I've ever done,' was Barney Walker's memory of the battle. 'It could have gone any way. The closest racing came 30 miles from the finish where the five yachts just wouldn't give up. The crews were all on deck and exhausted. The crew who made a mistake lost out big-time. We were hunting for every wind shift and covering every move.'

It was as though this was a five-boat match race, not a round-the-world marathon. It came down to the last 2 miles of the 1075 miles of racing to decide an incredible contest, which was made even more remarkable by the reception the fleet received as they approached Volvo's home town of Gothenburg in the middle of the night. 'It was amazing,' said Gordon Maguire. 'I've never seen anything like it. There were between 300 and 500 boats out there; every boat had a little white light on it. It was just a sea of little white lights.'

That sea of lights made it more difficult for the crews of the front five to spot the opposition and make sure they were well covered. Just after midnight on the fifth day it was *ASSA ABLOY* that emerged from the spectator fleet to claim first place, but only by 2 minutes, 16 seconds from *Tyco*, with *Team News Corp* just 1 minute, 40 seconds back in third place. And within an almost unbelievable 6 minutes, 50 seconds of *ASSA ABLOY* arriving, *illbruck* and *Amer Sports One* had also arrived. The reception was tumultuous.

Effervescent Magnus Olsson, one of Sweden's most famous ocean sailors, and watch leader aboard *ASSA ABLOY*, could hardly contain himself as the yacht approached the dock. With arms held firmly above his head and an indelible grin he shouted, 'What a great race. Better than any sailing I've ever done in my life. Great waves, lots of wind, big tidal changes, rocks, sandbanks, tacking all the time, boats everywhere, no sleep, adrenaline rushing. It was crazy, crazy, crazy. All the teams on the first five boats will remember this as a special day in their lives.'

The result made for a grandstand finish on the final leg of the circumnavigation. *illbruck* could still be beaten by *ASSA ABLOY*, and with *Team News Corp*, *Tyco* and *Amer Sports One* tied on points, whichever of those yachts was first home into Kiel would take third overall. The points table read *illbruck* 54, *ASSA ABLOY* 49, *Amer Sports One* 40, *Team News Corp* 40, *Tyco* 40, *SEB* 29, *djuice dragons* 25, *Amer Sports Too* 11.

≪ The crowded start of the final
leg of the VOR left little room
to move off Gothenburg.
Richard Langdon/Ocean Images

GOTHENBURG
TO KIEL

If you dare to dream you can expect a few

nightmares along the way.

JEZ FANSTONE — SKIPPER, *TEAM NEWS CORP*

after nine months and more than 32 000 nautical miles of racing around the planet, the Volvo Ocean Race had come down to a 220-mile sprint — less than 1 per cent of the total distance — to decide the outcome. And, ironically, while every competing sailor had put their life on the line sailing in horrendous conditions on some of the world's most dangerous oceans, the final stage from Gothenburg to Kiel in northern Germany was destined to be little more than a cruise across a near-windless pond.

Ten superbly sunny and warm days in Gothenburg helped to make it one of the more memorable port stopovers. Not surprisingly, since Volvo's international headquarters is located in the town, local support was exceptional. The yachts were based at Eriksberg, where a one-time ship drydock facility had been converted into a large floating marina. Over 100 000 people crammed into the venue to see the yachts over the one weekend they were in town.

It was during this stopover that Volvo confirmed the future of the race — it would be staged again in 2005/2006. The race's chief executive, Helge Alten, said that media coverage for Volvo had exceeded every expectation. The cumulative international television audience topped 650 million viewers, there had been nearly 13 000 stories published around the world and the event website had been logged on to by nearly three million visitors.

As impressive as the figures were, the 2001/2002 race still had one leg to go and the only figures the crews were interested in were those on the scoreboard. For Volvo, the decision to apply the same amount of points to every stage and not give a bonus for the longer courses had certainly kept the race alive. There were two important contests to be decided on Leg Nine — first and third. *illbruck* and *ASSA ABLOY* would battle for first, while *Amer Sports One*, *Team News Corp* and *Tyco* would go for third.

The yachts were lifted out of the water by crane onto the dockside at Eriksberg so the shore teams could complete thorough inspections of the rig and equipment, and give the hulls a final polish. Just prior to *Team News Corp* being hauled out, a serious gash about one metre long was discovered on the starboard bow at the waterline — the result of a solid impact with something during the leg from La Rochelle. Incredibly, the crew could not recall hitting anything, and concluded that it must have happened during the rough weather.

All sailing teams set about analysing every piece of meteorological information available and studying the tricky course that meandered through the islands of Denmark to Kiel. Some syndicates chartered aircraft to take key crewmembers on a familiarisation flight over the route.

The consensus was that the winds were going to be light, so some serious weight versus manpower calculations had to be made. Knut Frostad, bitterly disappointed by the performance of his *djuice dragons*, took the most extreme measure of all when it came to weight saving, opting to drop three crew and race with only nine on board. *Tyco* went with 11 and *Team News Corp* 10. Ross, Jez, Gordon and Barney decided that in the conditions the yacht could be effectively raced with the smaller crew, so they nominated Campbell Field and mid-deck hand Nigel King be dropped, primarily because they were the two heaviest crewmembers. The other change saw Peter Isler go aboard as tactician. Isler was training with Dennis Conner's America's Cup team off Long Beach in California when he got the call from Ross Field asking him to rejoin the team.

Jez:

> There's a chance there'll be a lot of racing rule protests on this leg so Peter's expertise with the rules will provide protection. His presence will give us the ability to get on with our job of sailing the boat and leave the technical issues to somebody else. Often when someone waves a protest flag at you, you don't know what rule they're claiming you breached. As a result there's a group discussion onboard for 15 minutes because everyone's a bit nervous ... and the boat goes slowly. We can now just turn around and say, 'OK, Peter, deal with it.'

In addition to a cutback in crew to save weight, *Team News Corp*, like every other race boat, was stripped of all excess equipment. Only one spinnaker pole would be carried and the absolute minimum number of sails went aboard. The toothpaste and dishwashing liquid was thrown away and for the first time in 32 000 miles there was no freeze-dried food — just 24 pizzas, some sandwiches and a few drinks for a race that was expected to take around 24 hours. Some of the crew even suggested that the team mascot and their unofficial 13th crewmember, the Bart Simpson doll, be left ashore because he was too fat. He stayed aboard.

It was as if Gothenburg had been blessed with fine weather for the stopover when yet another glorious day dawned for the start on 8 June. But there was an almost eerie atmosphere around the dock at Eriksberg as the yachts were being prepared. There were only a few thousand spectators present when tens of thousands were expected to see the fleet depart the dock. Soon, however, it would become evident where the rest of the spectators were.

Interviewed on the dock before heading out, *illbruck*'s John Kostecki admitted there were a few butterflies flitting around in his stomach: 'For sure there are a few nerves, but there are always nerves. I think it is important to have nerves to keep the competitive juices up.' He said he had decided to race with a full complement because 'the extra crew would be good movable ballast for the conditions', adding that, 'towards the end of the race there may be some upwind and light air sailing and on these boats you need a full crew to tack them. They're quite difficult to tack and manoeuvre.'

Neal McDonald was realistic about the task ahead of *ASSA ABLOY*. 'There's no doubt about it, it's a long shot for us — we're up against it. It's all about making sure that if opportunities arise we take them and use them to our benefit. The ultimate goal is still the same; we've got to try to win the race.'

Military jets gave a low-level aerobatic performance and left colourful vapour trails as they arced overhead. At the same time flares and thousands of balloons went aloft as the eight yachts en route to the start motored slowly away from the dock and cruised under the nearby bridge marking the entrance to Gothenburg Harbour. As they moved onto the waters of the archipelago none of the sailors were prepared for the sight that greeted them. It was almost beyond comprehension. Some 100 000 people had packed the shoreline and the mass of small, low-profile rocky isles of the archipelago, making each one look like a mid-ocean grandstand. And when it came to spectator boats the word armada was an understatement. There were at least 2500 small craft and commercial vessels plus two cruise liners out to watch the clash of the ocean warriors. These spectator boats were literally gunwale-to-gunwale across the narrow course area set through the chain of islands, leaving the sailors in no doubt that their exodus, while exciting, was not going to be easy, especially since there was only 8 knots of wind from the east.

At 2pm the start cannon was fired from the rampart of Älvsborgson Island, spinnakers were hoisted and mayhem ensued as the VOR yachts set out on the final leg of their journey. Maritime officials worked wonders in keeping the way ahead relatively clear, but behind the yachts, within metres of their transoms, came the aquatic equivalent of a cavalry charge. The waters turned into a blanket of white as engines on the spectator boats were engaged and the exit parade commenced. It was like eight swans being pursued by a thousand cygnets.

The *illbruck* team mastered the conditions superbly, harnessing the light breeze in their spinnaker and quickly moving into the lead. The seven other yachts were locked in a fight, gybing and criss-crossing behind *illbruck*, often having no option but to sail among the spectator boats in a bid to find a stable breeze. Kostecki's crew in the meantime were going their own way in clear wind, delivering an awesome display of light-weather sailing.

illbruck ghosted away while the others were kept back, restrained by a calm, a void created between the fading land breeze and the building sea breeze. Eventually the onshore breeze filled in, spinnakers were lowered and the pursuit of *illbruck* — already more than a mile ahead — commenced in earnest. *SEB* was the second yacht to pass the Trubaduren lighthouse at the outer limit of the archipelago, followed by *Team News Corp* — which had its challengers for third place overall, *Amer Sports One* and *Tyco*, well covered.

Once free from the clutches of the land the first true tactical decision came into play — which side of Anholt Island to take, west or east? Anholt, a low and long island measuring 15 miles by 7 miles, lay in the middle of the course to Store Strait, the passage that divides Denmark. By the time they reached Anholt and a commitment was called for, *Team SEB*, *Team News Corp* and *Tyco* had taken a dominant position over the fleet by moving out to the west. They had claimed *illbruck*, and *SEB* was in the lead.

Matt Humphries — navigator, *Team News Corp*

After a very tricky start the fleet has spread out, hoping that their wind information will be correct. Clearly, there are differing opinions and we hope we're right. Along with Tyco *and* SEB *we are in the west while the rest of the fleet is to the east as we approach Anholt. Presently we are sailing upwind under Code Zero in a very flat sea and under clear skies. We are expecting the wind to become quite variable tonight before settling in from the east.*

Minds were made up; the roulette wheel had been spun. Which side would win — west or east? It was a move that would decide the quest for third place in the race overall. *Amer Sports One* had nothing to lose at that stage and went east, while *illbruck's* crew opted to keep *ASSA ABLOY* covered on the eastern side of the island, too.

As they were in the high northern latitudes, this was close to being the land of the midnight sun. The sun only set for about five hours and the western sky never became fully dark, so there were just a few hours of darkness during which visual contact between the yachts might be lost. There was little opportunity to wriggle free unnoticed, except when an island lay between you and the opposition. Ten hours into the race there was a distance of only 3 miles between the eight boats in terms of the distance left to sail to the finish. The surprise was that *djuice* — now referred to by the crew as *'djuice light'* — was the leader.

Knut Frostad — skipper, *djuice dragons*

We've taken off anything we don't need to have for the rules. The boat is completely empty inside. Just a couple of sails, and nine crewmembers. So far it has paid off. When the wind died prior to rounding Anholt Island we felt fast and sailed away from Amer Sports One. Right now, the sun has just gone down and we've sailed a little away from illbruck and ASSA ABLOY. The next sked is certainly going to be exciting as the wind has shifted to the southeast, which means we should be better positioned than the guys who went on the west side of Anholt. Passing the sandbanks on the east side of Anholt was quite scary. We went as close as we dared and skirted the banks with just a foot of water under the [keel] bulb. I just really, really, really hope these conditions stay so we can be competitive all the way to the end.

When the sun began to surface from below the horizon there was visual confirmation of what the crews in the west already knew. They had blown it.

Peter Isler — tactician, *Team News Corp*

It all seemed to be going famously as the 'midnight sun' slowly faded towards the horizon. We had the westerly lane, along with SEB and Tyco, and a 15-mile-wide obstruction — the island of Anholt — right in front of us. But despite the best-laid plans, things can go wrong. The rest of the pack that went around Anholt to the east side sailed a much greater distance than we did, but they benefited from a favourable wind angle, making up for most of the extra distance.

Then, a few hours after rounding Anholt, calamity set in for the good guys out to the west. As we sailed towards the Danish shore the wind dropped off and headed us [changed direction towards the bow], so we could no longer steer our desired course. Worse than that, there soon wasn't enough wind for us to make headway against a foul current, so we had to anchor for two hours. SEB and Tyco *were nearby and anchored too. But the group to the east never stopped, and that put us where we are now ... hoping for another parking lot to even things out. Lately we've been making some inroads on the leaders, so we hope our good fortune can continue, but there aren't many passing lanes or any more 15-mile-wide islands to use to our advantage.*

'It's a bit depressing when the most powerful weapon in your inventory is your anchor,' was Jez's comment. 'That really did it for us. We were firmly rooted to the earth's crust while the other boats were sailing away.' Still, as Barney Walker explained, the crew remained positive: 'There was still a lot of eternal optimism on board. The guys were saying, "It'll be alright, we still have 100 miles to go and the race is a total lottery." We thought that if there was a God he would let us have one more shot at it. We soon realised God had a sick sense of humour that day.'

Ten miles ahead of both *Tyco* and *Team News Corp, Amer Sports One* was looking unbeatable for third overall. It was the same for *illbruck* over *ASSA ABLOY*, a situation that prompted navigator Mark Rudiger to write from *ASSA* that the crew were glad their fate as a race winner didn't hinge on the last leg. *illbruck* had them well covered, but still the pressure remained: the tactician couldn't rest, as this insight from *illbruck* revealed.

Ed Adams — tactician, *illbruck*

I've been trying to write this email for nearly a day now, but there's simply been too much happening. The wind has gone through nearly 360 degrees twice, gone completely calm three times, and there have been big islands and small shoals lying on the rhumb line [the direct course to the finish]. I'd start writing the email but then Stu [Bannatyne] would be on the intercom: 'Ed, could you please update us as to the status on our relative position to ASSA?' *You stop the email, and get on the radar. Tracking* ASSA ABLOY *is a full-time job. It's essential because our* only tactic for this race is to cover them no matter where they go. Every five minutes we log their range and bearing and analyse the relative gain or loss. Wait a minute ... it's Crusty [Mark Christensen] again. 'Ed, what's our average COG [course over ground] been lately? And what's the wind angle likely to be on the next course?'

Back to the email. We thought we had ASSA ABLOY put away after our breakaway start out of Gothenburg Harbour, but ASSA is fast and she quickly sailed from last place to just behind us when the breeze shut off at Anholt. Hold it, now Juan [Vila] is asking, 'Ed, can you check the tide set and drift strip charts and compare them to the tide model?'

Three minutes later ... back to the email. We were lucky the fleet split at Anholt as it was obvious only one side could pay a dividend (Which side? I don't think anyone was 100 per cent sure). We covered ASSA ABLOY, and the three boats that split to the other side (Tyco, News Corp and SEB) got dropped 15 miles back when the sea breeze swung through the south. If it had swung through the north our group would have been dropped. We're about 35 miles from the finish, in second place and still covering ASSA ABLOY. Every hour we pick up more and more spectator boats. We are now surrounded ... uh oh, here comes JK [John Kostecki], bounding down the companionway with more energy than seems humanly possible considering he's had only two hours' sleep in the past 24. 'Ed, do you have the latest sked (it arrives every hour)? What's the time to the layline? What are the wind readings ahead? Any new models, and how about radar and satellite pictures?'

I hand him the keyboard (it's quicker that way). JK continues, 'Why haven't you been on deck to look at the clouds lately?' I start heading for the deck and he calls me

*back, 'You know we have to do a boat email. When are
you going to do that?'*

djuice dragons remained the big surprise, holding a 4-mile lead when the coast of Kiel came into sight. And another surprise — the female crew aboard *Amer Sports Too* were leading their boss, Grant Dalton, aboard *Amer Sports One*. That gave Dalton something painful to contemplate as it was revealed that he was the one who, during a previous race, suggested that if a female crew ever beat him to the finish he would walk naked through the main street of Auckland with a pineapple firmly planted in his rectum.

The sailing remained frustrating for *SEB*, *Tyco* and *Team News Corp* as they made their way through Denmark's Store Strait. There were plenty of holes still to be found and in the end *Team News Corp* located the worst of them.

djuice managed to pick up a strengthening breeze before the opposition and sailed into Kiel mid-afternoon on 9 June to a massive welcome. The harbour was like a packed stadium with the crowd officially estimated at more than 100 000 lining the shore 20-deep to see the pink-and-black boat finish. More than 500 boats made up the on-water escort. For Knut Frostad there was finally some level of relief in what had been a frustrating campaign. His yacht, which hadn't fired for 99 per cent of the race, had cracked a win. And there was a bonus to come with the result — it forced *Team SEB* (which retired from two legs through rudder and mast failure) back to second-last on the overall points.

There was no denying that the real reason so many people had converged on Kiel was to see their nation's entry, *illbruck*, claim the outright victory. And they weren't to be robbed of the experience. The green-and-white boat sailed to the finish line amid unprecedented scenes of celebration. The clear-cut pre-race favourite had lived up to all expectations in superb fashion and was the worthy winner of the 2001/2002 Volvo Ocean Race. But despite the jubilation around him skipper John Kostecki remained as he had throughout the race, a man almost devoid of euphoria. Grasping the champion's crystal trophy he looked distinctly uncomfortable as he tried to find his own level of excitement to match the celebrations. He took time to again thank his team and said that in the light and variable conditions they were never certain until the final few miles that they would win. Beyond that he was all but lost for words.

For Neal McDonald and the *ASSA ABLOY* team their remote chance of displacing *illbruck* at the top of the podium never went close to eventuating. However, considering their results on the first two legs, *ASSA ABLOY* improved the most out of all the racers. It was an outstanding team effort.

Leg Nine continued to be full of surprises when Lisa McDonald's *Amer Sports Too* beat *Amer Sports One* into fourth place — their best result in the entire race. Grant Dalton arrived at the dock and immediately received a pineapple as a gift from the girls. The smooth end of the situation for him was that *Amer Sports One* was third outright.

For *Team News Corp* the result on the leg could not have been worse as they trailed behind *SEB* and *Tyco* into port, having 'parked' in two calms off the Danish coast. A small consolation was the welcome they received as Bluey, their nickname for the yacht, crawled towards the line in near-windless conditions with the 'drifter' headsail set. It was almost midnight but around 5000 people remained to cheer them home while nearly 100 boats guided them in. The gun firing to signal their arrival was the cue for flares to go up and thunderous cheering to prevail. The last boat was home and the final curtain had come down on the race.

The crew were gutted by the result. 'It's probably been the most depressing 36 hours of yacht racing in our respective careers,' said Jez, 'but it's been nine months of fun, excitement and sheer joy to sail with these guys. I guess the last 36 hours is really a small price to pay for the experience. As I've always said, if you dare to dream you can expect a few nightmares along the way.'

As Jez stepped off *Team News Corp* for the last time and stood on the dock, he looked back at the boat that had taken the team around the world safely and said, 'Goodbye Bluey. You've been a great bus.' He and the rest of the boys in blue disappeared into the night, destined to party until the sun was well above the horizon. Their party venue was a large motor yacht moored nearby. As the drinks started to flow and the pain of the final leg eased slightly, Gordon spoke philosophically of the result: 'I'm experiencing a little bit of denial because the result is really devastating. We didn't deserve it, so you don't really want to get too mixed up in the emotion of it. I keep telling myself that the sun will come up tomorrow, and my wife and kids will still love me tomorrow, and that the world will continue to go around. But somehow, right now, it just doesn't feel right.'

FINAL POINTS

1 *illbruck Challenge* 61
2 *ASSA ABLOY* 55
3 *Amer Sports One* 44
4 *Team Tyco* 42
5 *Team News Corp* 41
6 *djuice dragons* 33
7 *Team SEB* 32
8 *Amer Sports Too* 16

Top Shore crew and supporters welcome *Team News Corp* as it approaches the dock in Kiel after 32 700 nautical miles and nine months of racing. More than 5000 people thronged the shore to greet the yacht.

Centre Glad it's all over but bitterly disappointed with the final result, the *Team News Corp* crew arrives in Kiel.

Bottom Cham-pain. Skipper Jez Fanstone takes a swig of champagne to celebrate the end of the race while contemplating what might have been.

All images *Richard Langdon/Ocean Images*

Epilogue

It is the wind, that invisible and uncontrollable force, that generates the magical appeal bringing people from all walks of life together on common ground — under sail. To race a sailboat is to be in harmony with nature, knowing all the time you will never beat it, only match it.

In sailing, you can have the best yacht, the best equipment and the world's best crew, but you can lose a race by a significant margin because the key ingredient, the weather, did not go your way. In the 2001/2002 Volvo Ocean Race it was never more evident that sailing, more than any other sport, can be a game of luck — and it teaches you how to lose.

Crewmembers from all the competing yachts held vivid memories of moments during the previous nine months that classified them as true ocean warriors. It was on the Southern Ocean legs in particular that potential catastrophe prowled day and night. The vast majority confirmed that the most disconcerting part of the race was careering through fields of growlers and icebergs knowing that luck, more often than great sailing skills, was dealing with their fate.

That element of luck was never better revealed than in *Team SEB*'s terrifying experience in the Southern Ocean. It was night and the yacht was in turmoil during a massive storm, lying on its side, dismasted, the interior filling with torrents of icy cold water while waves crashed over the hull. Salvation was way beyond the influence of the crew — their fate lay in the hands of a greater power. The game could have gone either way, but this time the yacht came upright and remained afloat. Had that not happened, those 12 sailors might have perished.

The previous nine months of gruelling racing was certainly not reflected in the anticlimax of the final leg, which was dogged by light and variable conditions. The results showed that the race for third place — and the leg for that matter — was decided on the whim of the wind and mood of the current. As they watched *Amer Sports One* claim third place outright, the crews of both *Tyco* and *Team News Corp* could look back and say 'if only' they hadn't lost their respective rudders earlier in the race. At the same time, they accepted that such incidents are part of the game. Both teams acknowledged that *Amer Sports One* faced a far greater hurdle just to be in the event. Grant Dalton's syndicate was the last to line up for the race and they did their development work as they made their way around the planet.

Regardless of the weather, no one could take anything away from *illbruck*'s outright win. The adjectives 'impressive', 'well planned' and 'clearly superior' all aptly describe the achievement of John Kostecki and his carefully groomed team. They were methodical in their approach and flawless in the execution of their plan. And, considering the level of competition, theirs will be considered the most meritorious win ever in round-the-world racing. Incredibly, though, after sailing around the world this champion team stood the chance of being trapped by calms and unfavourable winds on that final leg and, as a consequence, being robbed of their well-deserved triumph ... beaten by a factor beyond their control.

It is the danger and the challenge associated with being taken to the edge of the precipice that bring many of the sailors back to this race time after time. It is an attitude that the majority of people struggle to comprehend as they go about their conventional day. For the VOR sailors and adventurers the world over, their answer can be found in the words of Australian poet, Adam Lindsay Gordon:

No game was ever worth a rap for a rational man to play
Into which no accident, no mishap, could possibly find its way.

Leaderboard

Standings at end of Leg Nine — Gothenburg to Kiel

	Yacht Name	Leg 9 Elapsed Time	Leg 9 Points	Total Points
1	*illbruck Challenge*	01d 04h 17m 45s	7	61
2	*ASSA ABLOY*	01d 06h 13m 40s	6	55
3	*Amer Sports One*	01d 06h 19m 30s	4	44
4	*Team Tyco*	01d 09h 27m 10s	2	42
5	*Team News Corp*	01d 10h 11m 50s	1	41
6	*djuice dragons*	01d 03h 42m 30s	8	33
7	*Team SEB*	01d 08h 01m 00s	3	32
8	*Amer Sports Too*	01d 06h 18m 10s	5	16

Standings at end of Leg Eight — La Rochelle to Gothenburg

	Yacht Name	Leg 8 Elapsed Time	Leg 8 Points	Total Points
1	*illbruck Challenge*	04d 7h 11m 55s	5	54
2	*ASSA ABLOY*	04d 7h 6m 38s	8	49
3	*Amer Sports One*	04d 7h 13m 28s	4	40
3	*Team News Corp*	04d 7h 10m 34s	6	40
3	*Team Tyco*	04d 7h 8m 54s	7	40
6	*Team SEB*	04d 7h 57m 50s	3	29
7	*djuice dragons*	04d 10h 19m 58s	2	25
8	*Amer Sports Too*	04d 18h 50m 35s	1	11

Standings at end of Leg Seven — Annapolis to La Rochelle

	Yacht Name	Leg 7 Elapsed Time	Leg 7 Points	Total Points
1	*illbruck Challenge*	010d 20h 44m 30s	8	49
2	*ASSA ABLOY*	010d 23h 39m 40s	7	41
3	*Amer Sports One*	011d 02h 04m 00s	4	36
4	*Team News Corp*	011d 02h 42m 40s	3	34
5	*Team Tyco*	011d 00h 19m 10s	6	33
6	*Team SEB*	011d 01h 53m 30s	5	26
7	*djuice dragons*	011d 08h 09m 00s	2	23
8	*Amer Sports Too*	Retired from Leg 7	1	10

Standings at end of Leg Six — Miami to Baltimore

	Yacht Name	Leg 6 Elapsed Time	Leg 6 Points	Total Points
1	*illbruck Challenge*	03d 14h 01m 44s	5	41
2	*ASSA ABLOY*	03d 13h 58m 44s	6	34
3	*Amer Sports One*	03d 13h 38m 48s	7	32
4	*Team News Corp*	03d 13h 12m 32s	8	31
5	*Team Tyco*	04d 01h 00m 18s	3	27
6	*Team SEB*	03d 21h 42m 23s	4	21
6	*djuice dragons*	04d 01h 10m 58s	2	21
8	*Amer Sports Too*	04d 01h 46m 34s	1	9

Standings at end of Leg Five — Rio de Janeiro to Miami

	Yacht Name	Leg 5 Elapsed Time	Leg 5 Points	Total Points
1	*illbruck Challenge*	17d 14h 21m 52s	7	36
2	*ASSA ABLOY*	17d 13h 19m 57s	8	28
3	*Amer Sports One*	17d 20h 47m 40s	3	25
4	*Team Tyco*	17d 14h 34m 15s	6	24
5	*Team News Corp*	17d 18h 26m 28s	4	23
6	*djuice dragons*	19d 00h 37m 50s	2	19
7	*Team SEB*	17d 17h 16m 20s	5	17
8	*Amer Sports Too*	19d 02h 33m 27s	1	8

Standings at end of Leg Four — Auckland to Rio de Janeiro

	Yacht Name	Leg 4 Elapsed Time	Leg 4 Points	Total Points
1	*illbruck Challenge*	23d 5h 58m 42s	8	29
2	*Amer Sports One*	23d 14h 50m 55s	4	22
3	*ASSA ABLOY*	23d 14h 22m 21s	5	20
4	*Team News Corp*	24d 21h 55m 10s	3	19
5	*Team Tyco*	23d 13h 4m 52s	6	18
6	*djuice dragons*	23d 11h 52m 42s	7	17
7	*Team SEB*	Retired from Leg 4	1	12
8	*Amer Sports Too*	25d 11h 06m 50s	2	7

Standings at end of Leg Three — Sydney to Auckland

	Yacht Name	Leg 3 Elapsed Time	Leg 3 Points	Total Points
1	*illbruck Challenge*	8d 14h 52m 41s	5	21
2	*Amer Sports One*	8d 13h 39m 6s	7	18
3	*Team News Corp*	8d 14h 54m 54s	4	16
4	*ASSA ABLOY*	8d 11h 50m 42s	8	15
5	*Team Tyco*	8d 14h 48m 39s	6	12
6	*Team SEB*	Retired from Leg 3	1	11
7	*djuice dragons*	8d 17h 46m 49s	3	10
8	*Amer Sports Too*	10d 5h 57m 52s	2	5

Standings at end of Leg Two — Cape Town to Sydney

	Yacht Name	Leg 2 Elapsed Time	Leg 2 Points	Total Points
1	*illbruck Challenge*	22d 13h 22m 26s	8	16
2	*Team News Corp*	22d 15h 17m 29s	6	12
3	*Amer Sports One*	22d 19h 50m 12s	4	11
4	*Team SEB*	22d 14h 35m 45s	7	10
5	*djuice dragons*	22d 19h 43m 35s	5	7
6	*ASSA ABLOY*	22d 22h 31m 05s	3	7
7	*Team Tyco*	Retired from Leg 2	1	6
8	*Amer Sports Too*	26d 4h 59m 22s	2	3

Standings at end of Leg One — Southampton to Cape Town

	Yacht Name	Leg 1 Elapsed Time	Leg 1 Points	Total Points
1	*illbruck Challenge*	31d 6h 19m 49s	8	8
2	*Amer Sports One*	31d 8h 20m 56s	7	7
3	*Team News Corp*	32d 15h 57m 17s	6	6
4	*Team Tyco*	33d 16h 37m 49s	5	5
5	*ASSA ABLOY*	34d 18h 11m 59s	4	4
6	*Team SEB*	36d 19h 35m 47s	3	3
7	*djuice dragons*	37d 5h 0m 53s	2	2
8	*Amer Sports Too*	37d 11h 20m 12s	1	1

Excerpt from Notice of Race, Appendix 2 (Scoring System) A2.2(f):
When there is a tie on total points between two or more boats, the tie will be broken in favour of the boat with the most points from first places, and, if the tie remains, the most points from second places, and so on. If after completing the procedures described above a tie still exists, it will be broken in favour of the boat that had the highest position on the last leg.